CARL LARSSON'S
Home, Family and Farm

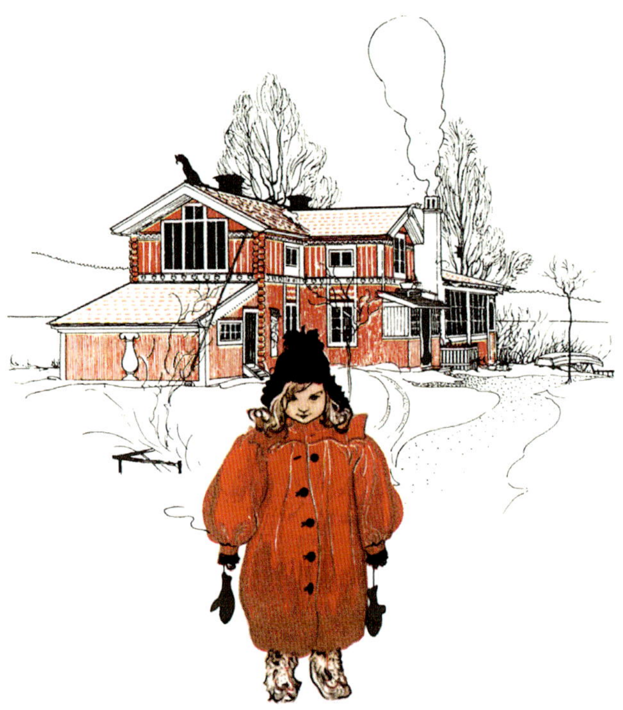

A Home, *A Family* and *A Farm* first published in Swedish by Albert Bonniers, Stockholm, as
Ett Hem (1899), *Carl Larsson – En Målare Och Hans Familj* (1979), and *Spadarvet* (1966), respectively
First published in English by G.P Putnam, New York in 1974, 1979 and 1976 respectively, and by
Methuen Children's Books, London in 1980 (*A Family*) and 1977 (*A Farm*)

This English version by Polly Lawson, based on original text by Lennart Rudström
First published individually by Floris Books in 2006, 2007 and 2008 respectively
This combined edition published 2014 by Floris Books. Fifth printing 2025

British Library CIP data available ISBN 978-178250-047-6 Printed in China through Imago

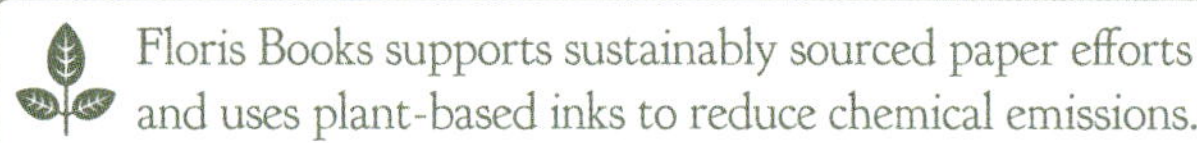

CARL LARSSON'S
Home, Family and Farm

PAINTINGS FROM THE SWEDISH ARTS AND CRAFTS MOVEMENT

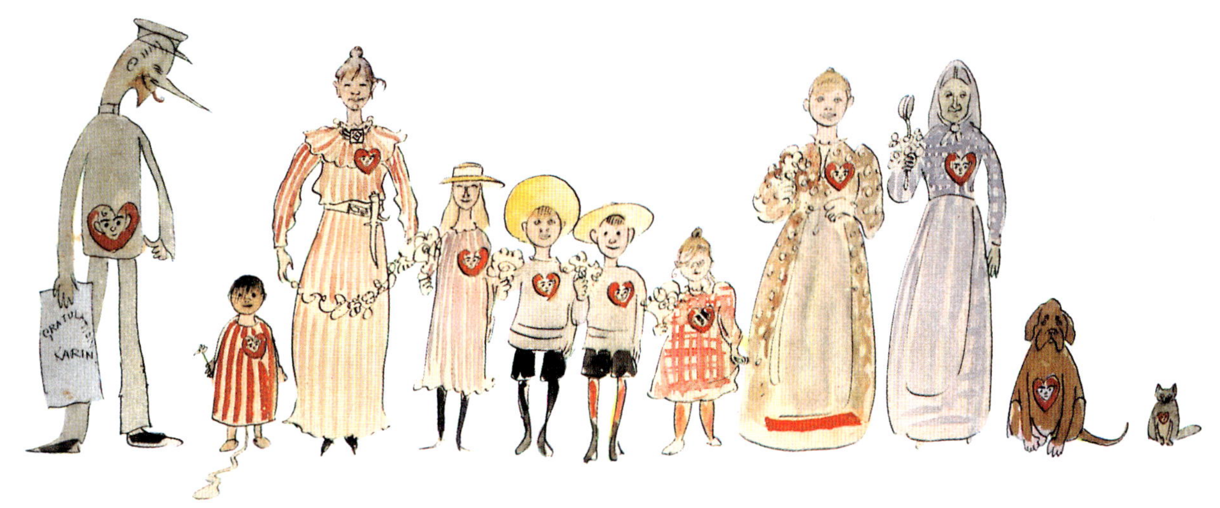

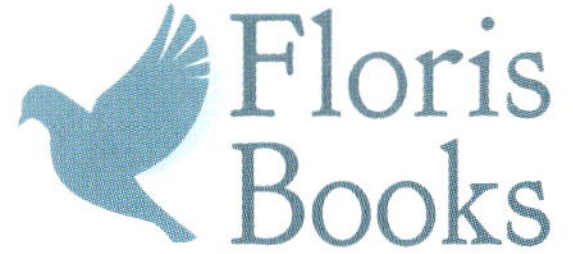

Floris Books

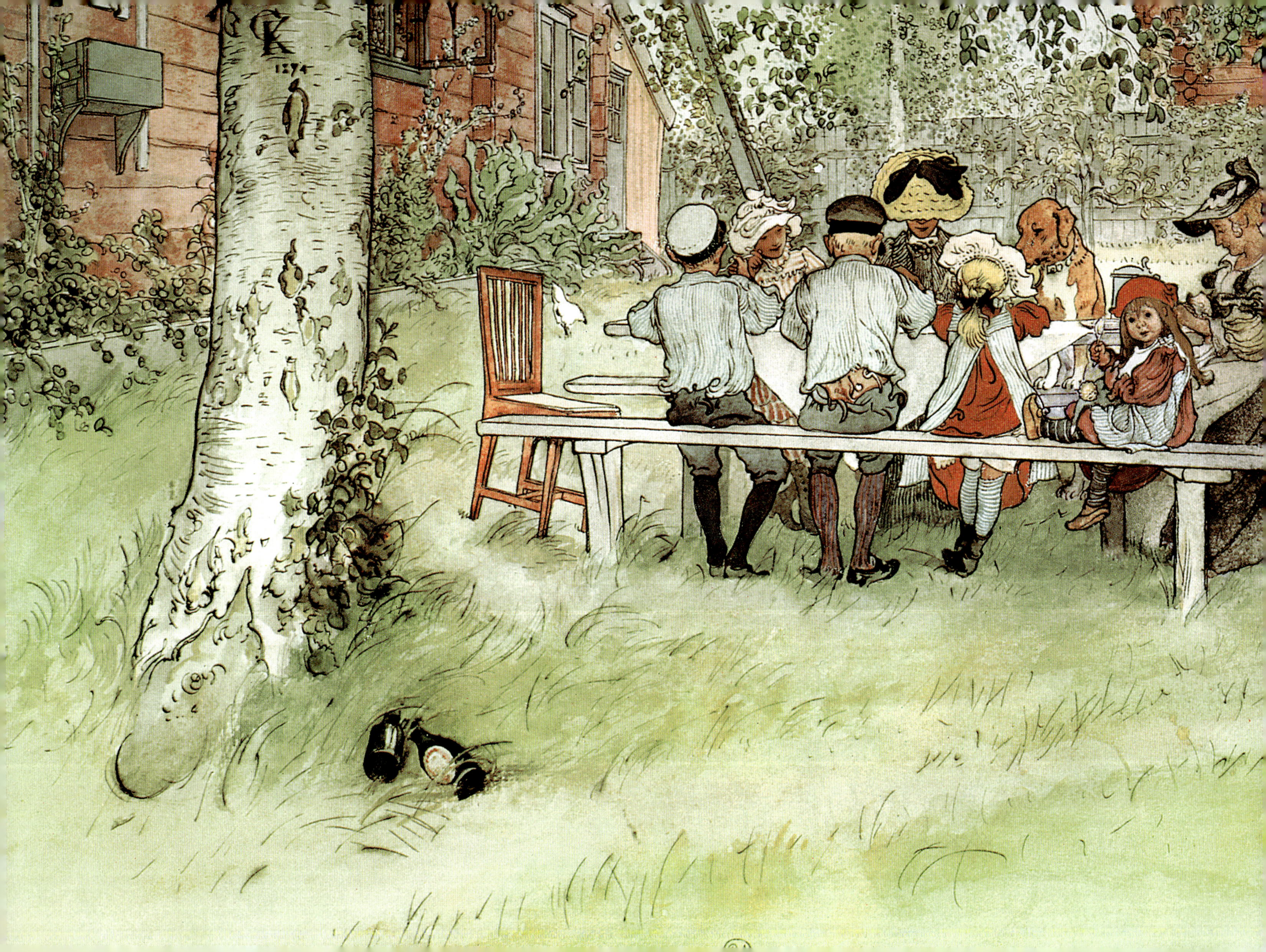

A HOME

Carl Larsson came to live in the small town of Sundborn in western Sweden in 1888, and it is from here that he drew the inspiration for his paintings.

His artistic techniques are well-documented. He would start by doing a sketch of the scene in pencil or India ink. All the paintings in this book were then finished in watercolour, leaving some areas blank so the paper shines through.

The bridge shown in this painting leads to a farm called Lilla Hyttnäs (The Little Hut on a Point). It was here that Carl and his wife Karin lived with their eight children.

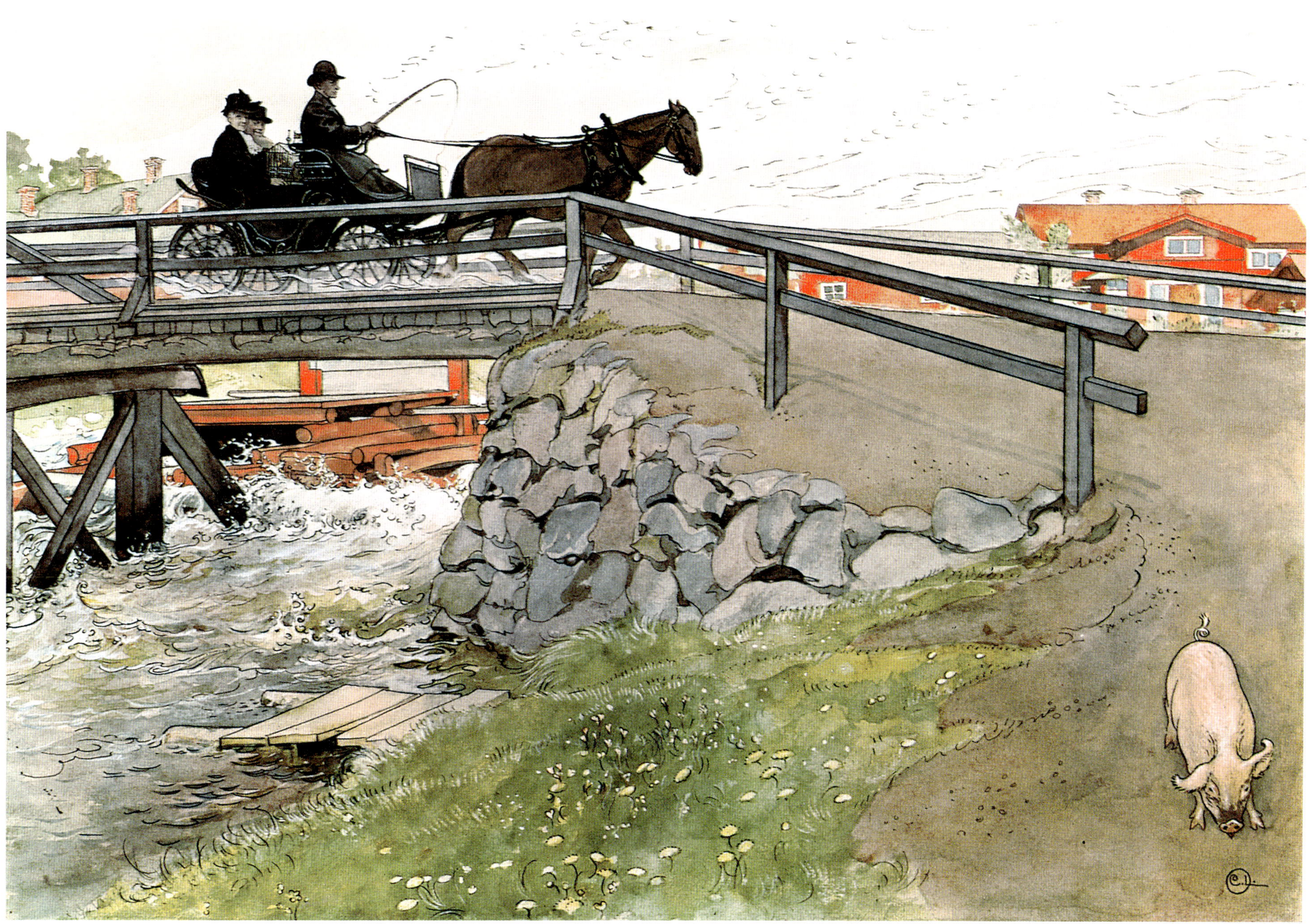

The Larssons' house, a two-storeyed cottage built in 1837, was a work in progress. The house was built on a waste ground, and when it was given to Carl and Karin by Karin´s father Adolf Bergöö, it was not in a good state of repair. They worked to improve it – over the years, seven major upgrades in all. One of the improvements Carl made to accommodate his ever-growing body of work was to add an artist's studio, seen here with a white chimney and a wall of windows. This allowed him to move on from painting small watercolours and oils to producing large-scale paintings.

This painting shows the untamed nature of the house. Some people in Sundborn thought it was an eyesore, with added rooms sticking out everywhere and hand-carved wooden dragons on the roof.

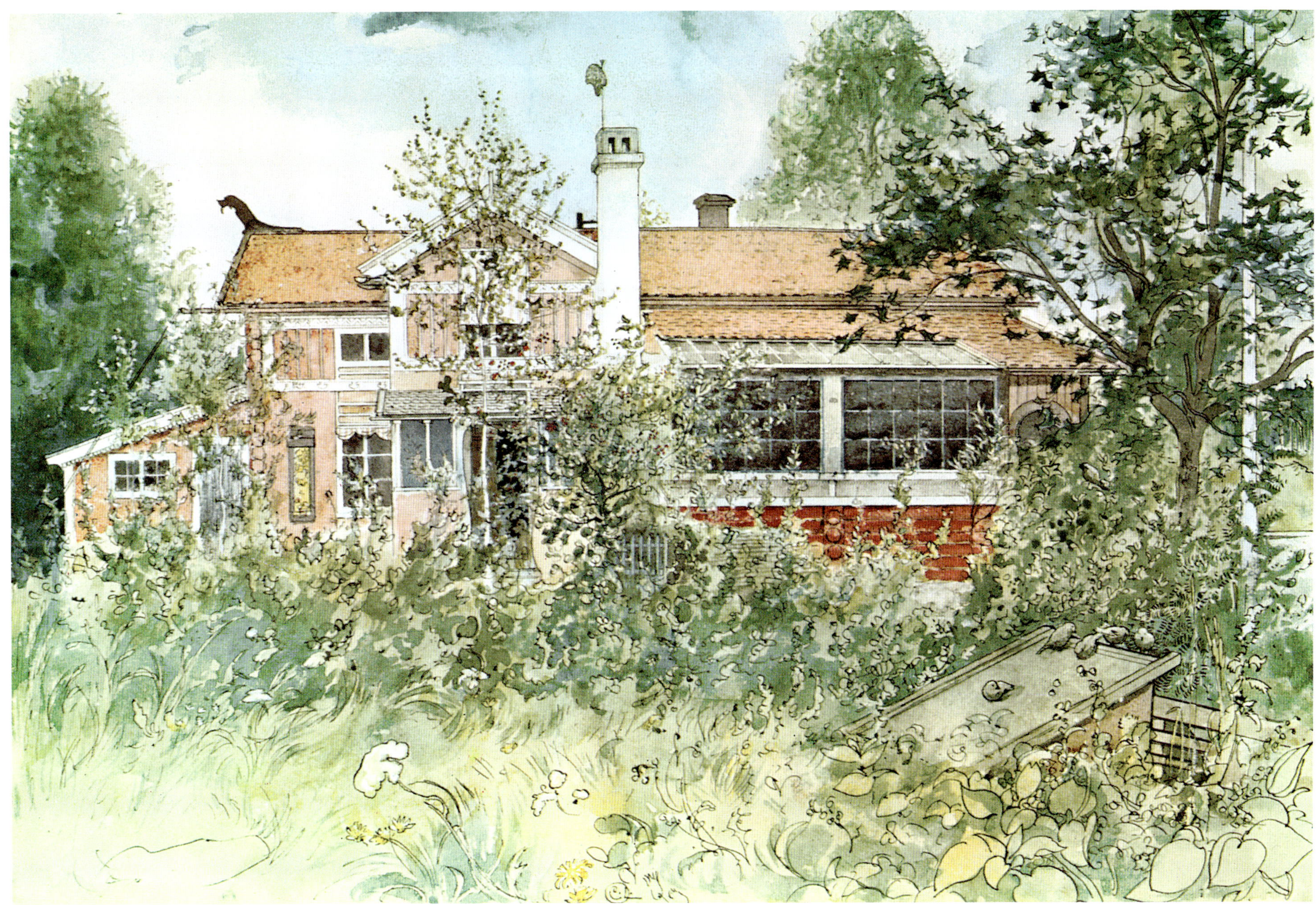

This painting shows Carl Larsson's studio from the inside. On the table is a paint box, along with paper, chalk and India ink. There's also a box of watercolours, and paintbrushes made from squirrel hair and marten's tail hair.

In the far right corner is his parasol, used for shading his canvas when working outdoors. The half-finished painting on the easel is probably of his daughter Lisbeth.

In addition to painting, Carl was an accomplished wood carver and carpenter. He created the dragons in the previous painting; he also enjoyed carving old men and birds. You can see his carpentry tools on the far wall: a saw, a plane, a chisel, a drill, a screwdriver and a ruler.

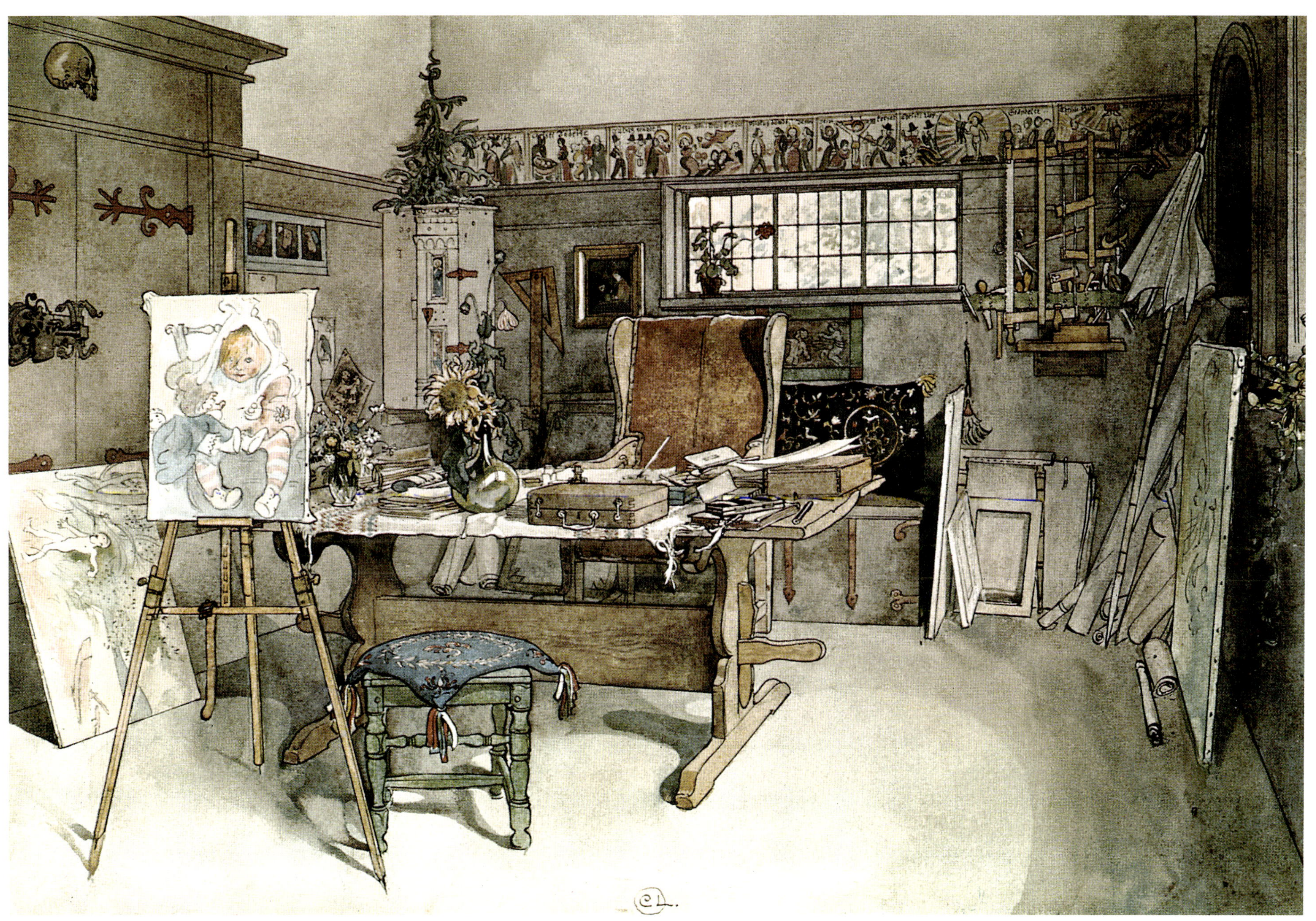

More of the studio is visible in this painting, looking in the other direction. The woman modelling for him was the Larssons' maid, Anna, and she would frequently sit for a week or two for a single painting.

Carl made the red sofa in the corner, an example of both his carpentry skills and quirky sense of humour: the angry red figure on top of the high post, leaning heavily on his stick, is Carl himself. There's also a door in the post leading to a small cupboard where he kept his oil paints; he wrote a list in pencil on the inside of the door indicating where each tube should go.

Ulf, one of Carl's sons, can be seen leaning out of the high window. The painting on the inside of the main door is of Karin.

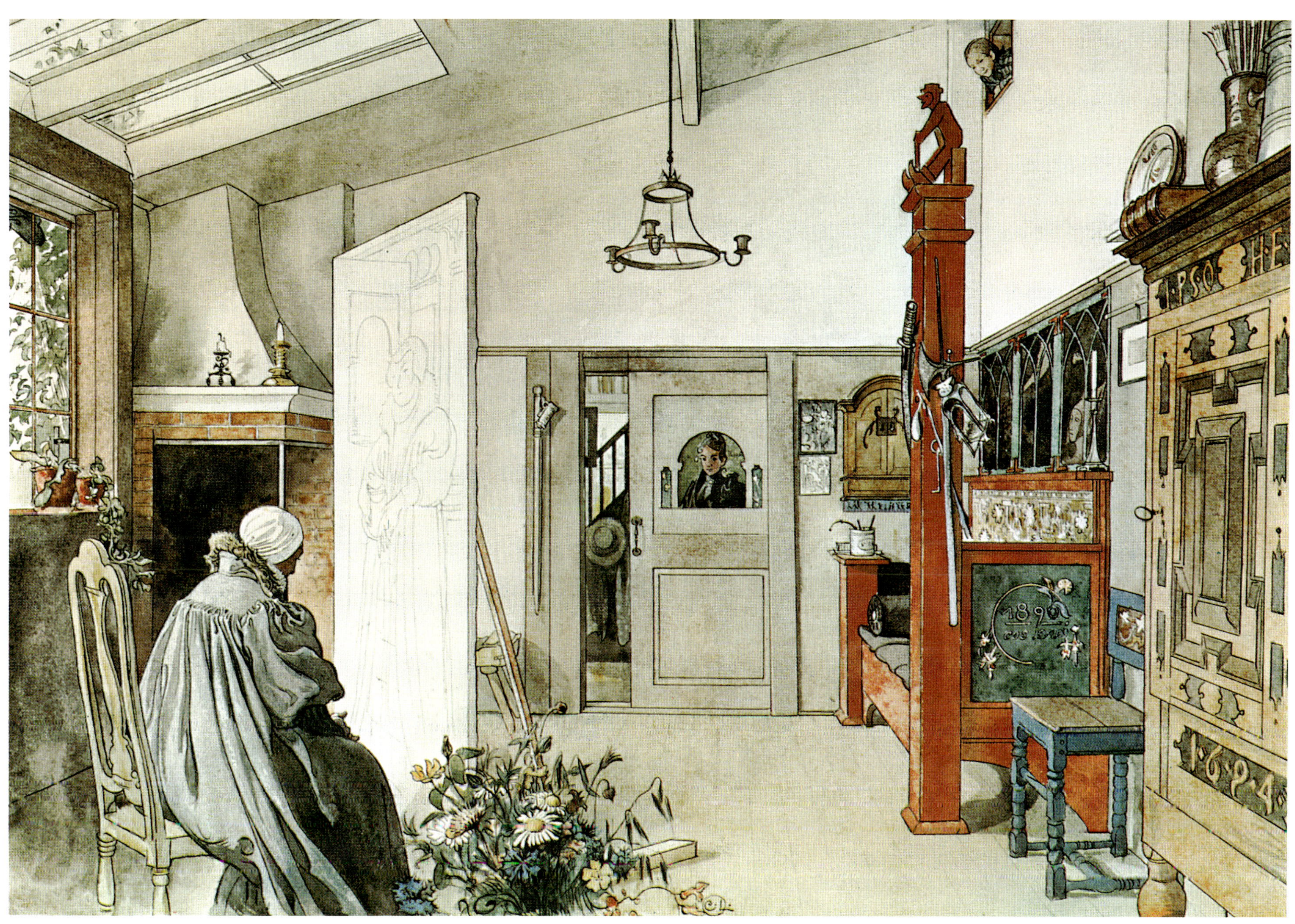

Karin and Carl would spend time together in the dining room, after the children had gone to bed.

They had first met in France, in a little village south of Paris called Grez where they had both gone to paint. One summer after they arrived in Sundborn, so the story goes, it rained every day for six weeks. Carl was very frustrated at not being able to paint outdoors, so Karin suggested that he should paint indoor things: the children, the flowers, the furniture, the scene from the window. That is how his life-long passion for interiors started.

Karin and Carl lived at Lilla Hyttnäs for thirty years.

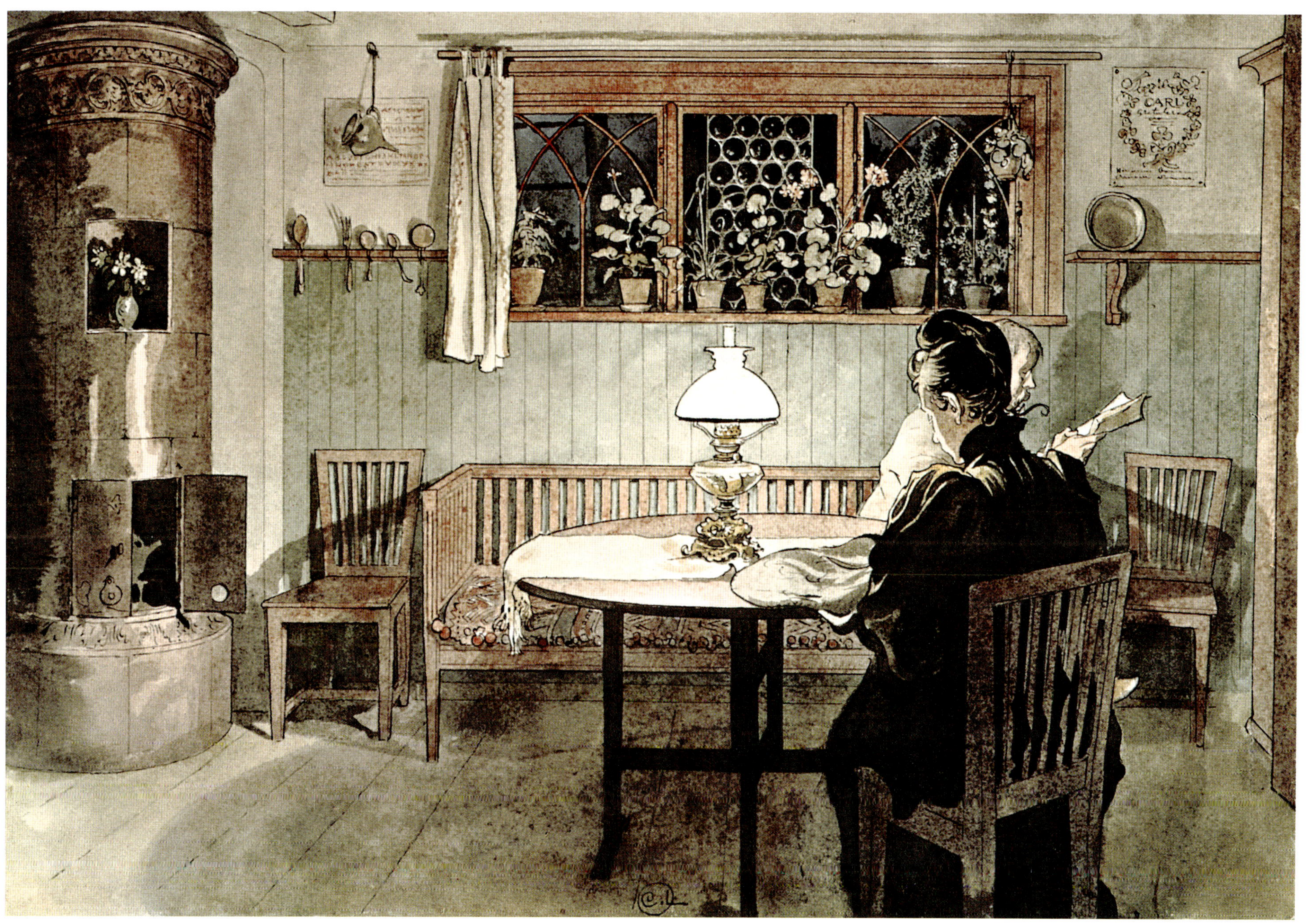

This was actually the first painting that Carl did after he started painting interiors. Known as "The Punishment Corner," it shows Carl's son Pontus being disciplined in the drawing room. Next to him is a highly decorated stove with tiles depicting birds, flowers and hearts. To Pontus's right, the door is inscribed in English: "There was a little woman, lived with C. L., and if she's not gone, she lives there still – very well." The rhyme refers to Karin, who is shown in the lower door panel.

As Carl's paintings grew popular in book-format, he became known not just as painter but as an innovative interior designer. The Swedish style of making your own brightly-painted furniture, and decorating panels and woodwork with drawings and inscriptions, is often attributed to him.

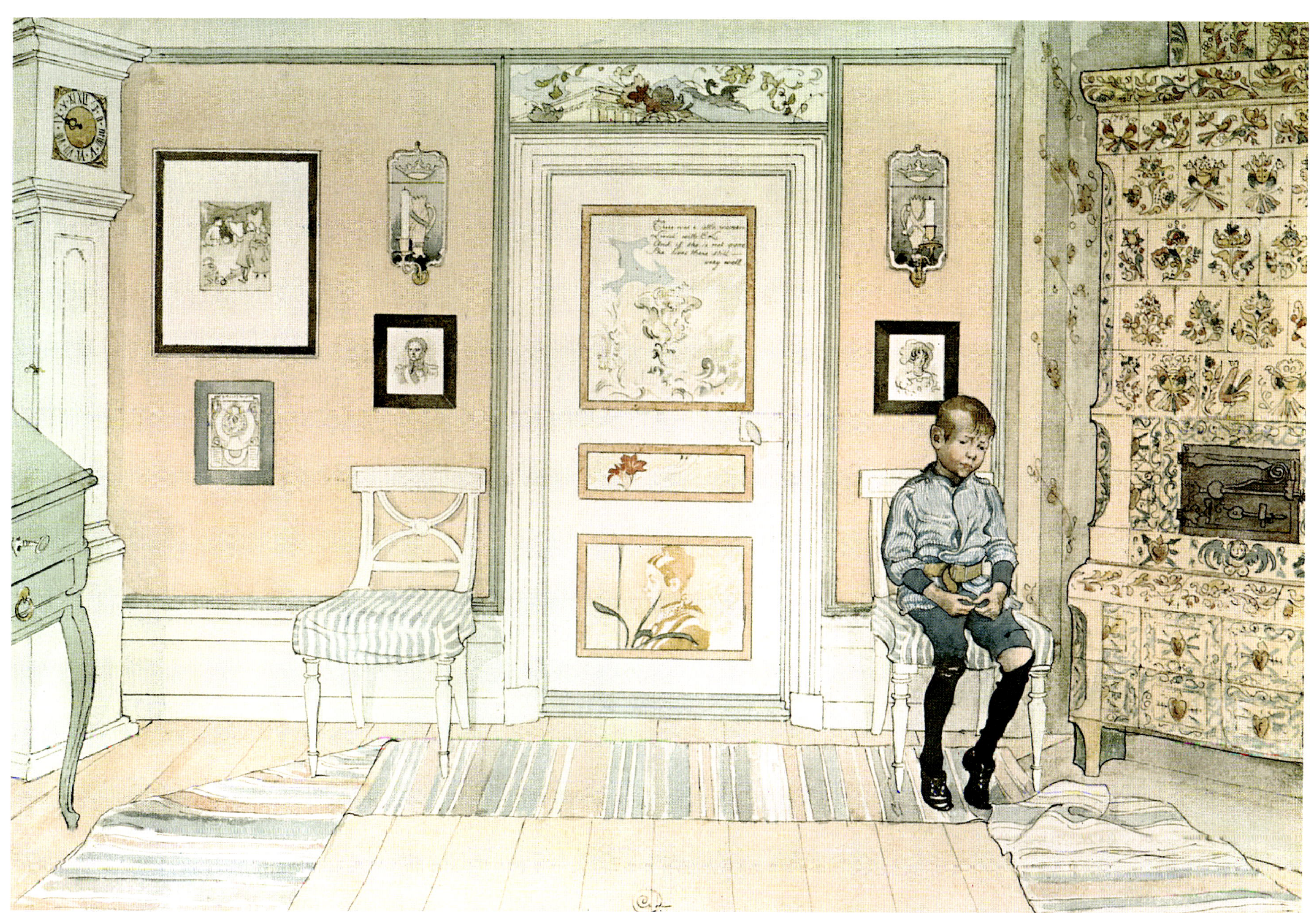
There was a little woman
Lived with Ek
And if she is not gone
She lives there still —
very well

This painting is also set in the drawing room, or parlour, and features Carl's daughter Suzanne. Most houses around the end of the nineteenth century were dark and gloomy, with everything in muted colours. Carl Larsson's house stood out because of its abundance of natural light and bright colours. Everything was painted: window-sills, panels and furniture, in blues, reds, whites and greens.

With eight children, Karin didn't have extended periods of time in which to paint, so she started weaving rugs and tapestries instead – the striped rug shown in this picture is hers. She adopted a geometric style in clear colours, quite different to Carl's approach. She would design her patterns with charcoal and chalk on wrapping paper, and pin them up behind the loom.

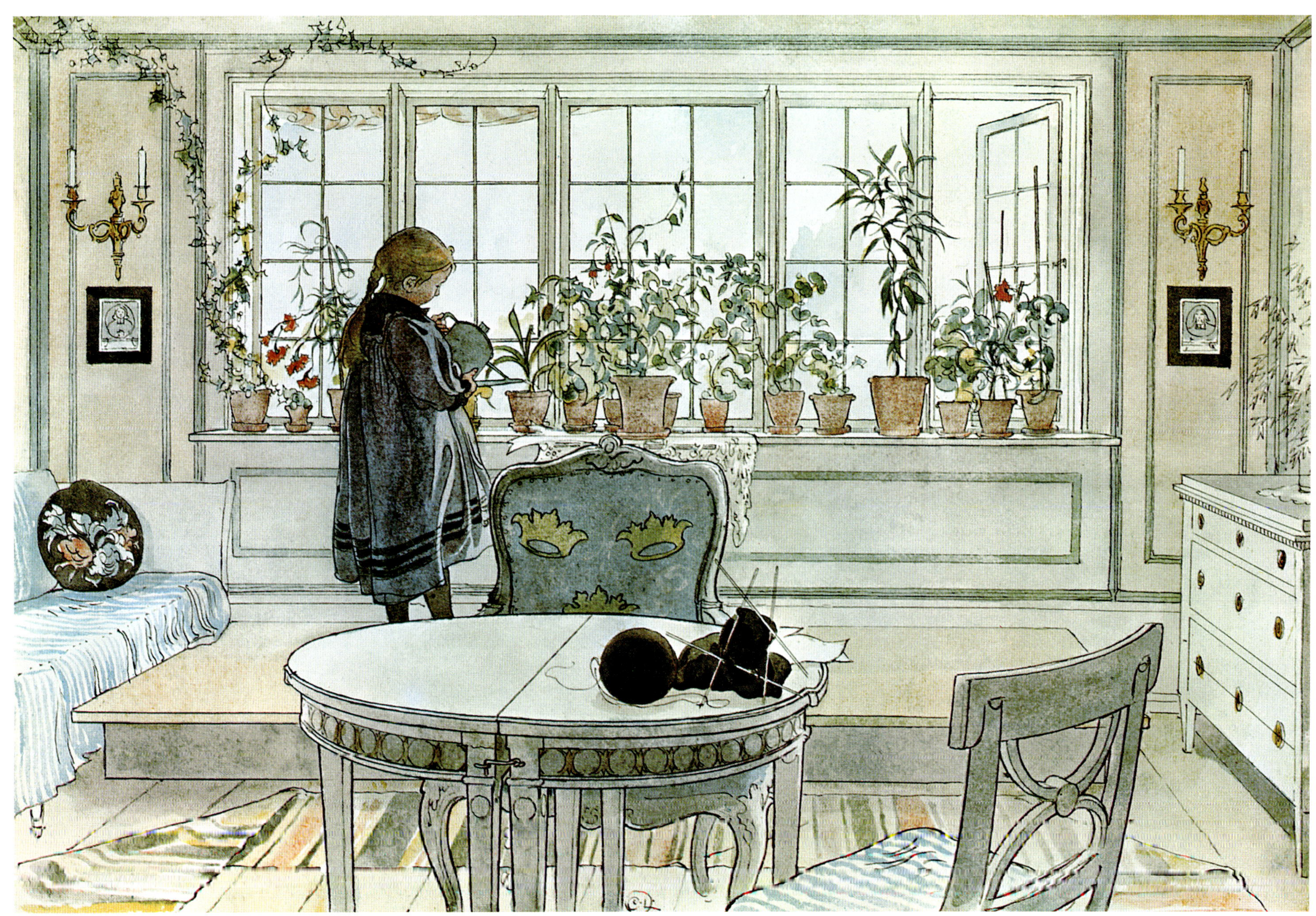

Here is another view of the Larssons' parlour; this painting is known as the "Lazy Corner" and features their dog, Kapo.

The sofa in the corner is where Carl liked to rest; the large pipe is his.

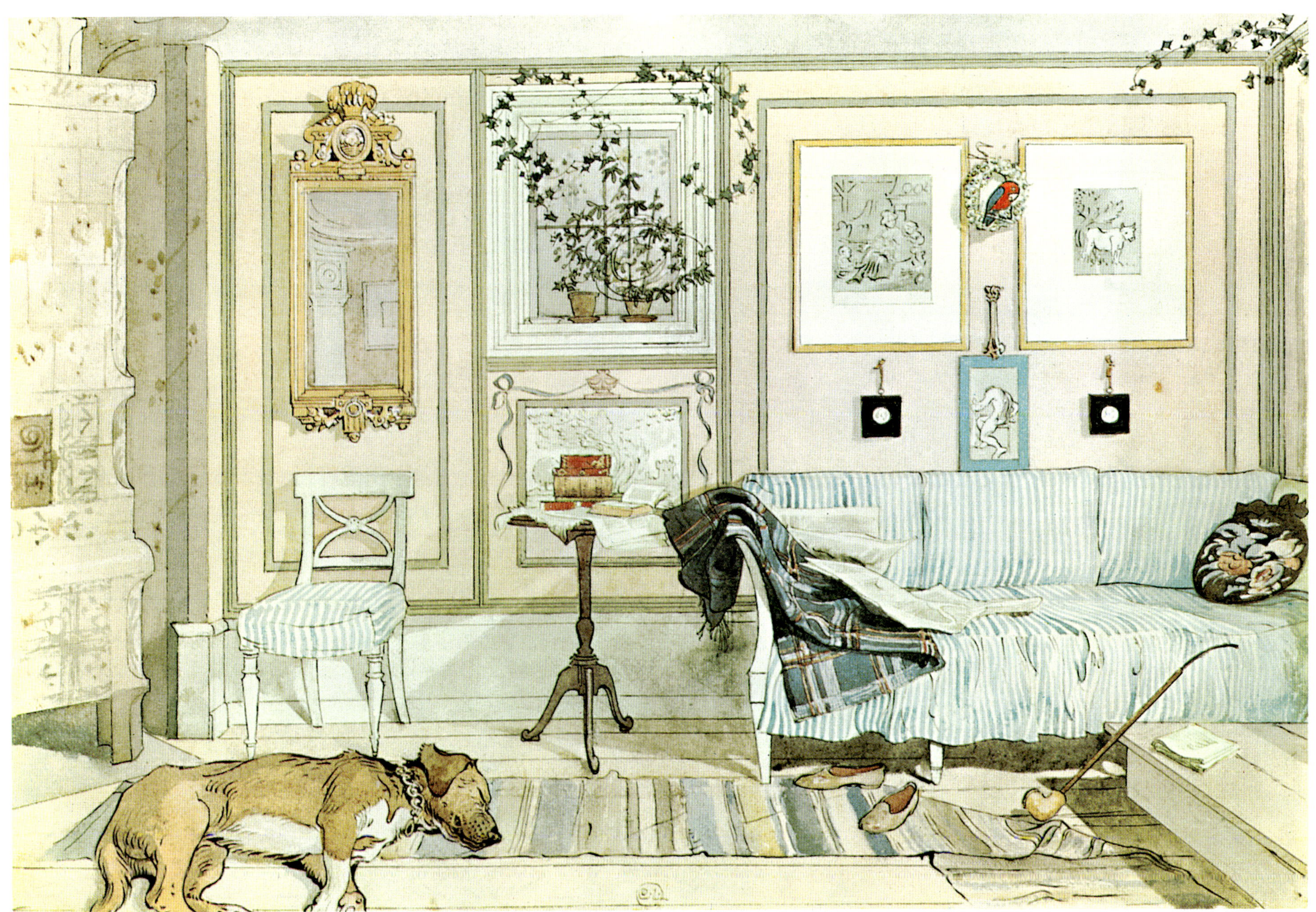

The kitchen was the one room that Carl didn't decorate. There had been a big stone fireplace on the right, where the kitchen range is in this painting, but it was torn down one summer when the family were away to make way for the modern range and a steel hood. Carl was furious and reclaimed the stone to make a table and bench in the garden.

On the left you can see the green spice chest which would have contained thyme, majoram, cloves, ginger, mint, chervil, vanilla and much more. The family's cook, Emma, was responsible for keeping the copper pans on the stove brightly polished. Here, Suzanne and Kersti are churning butter.

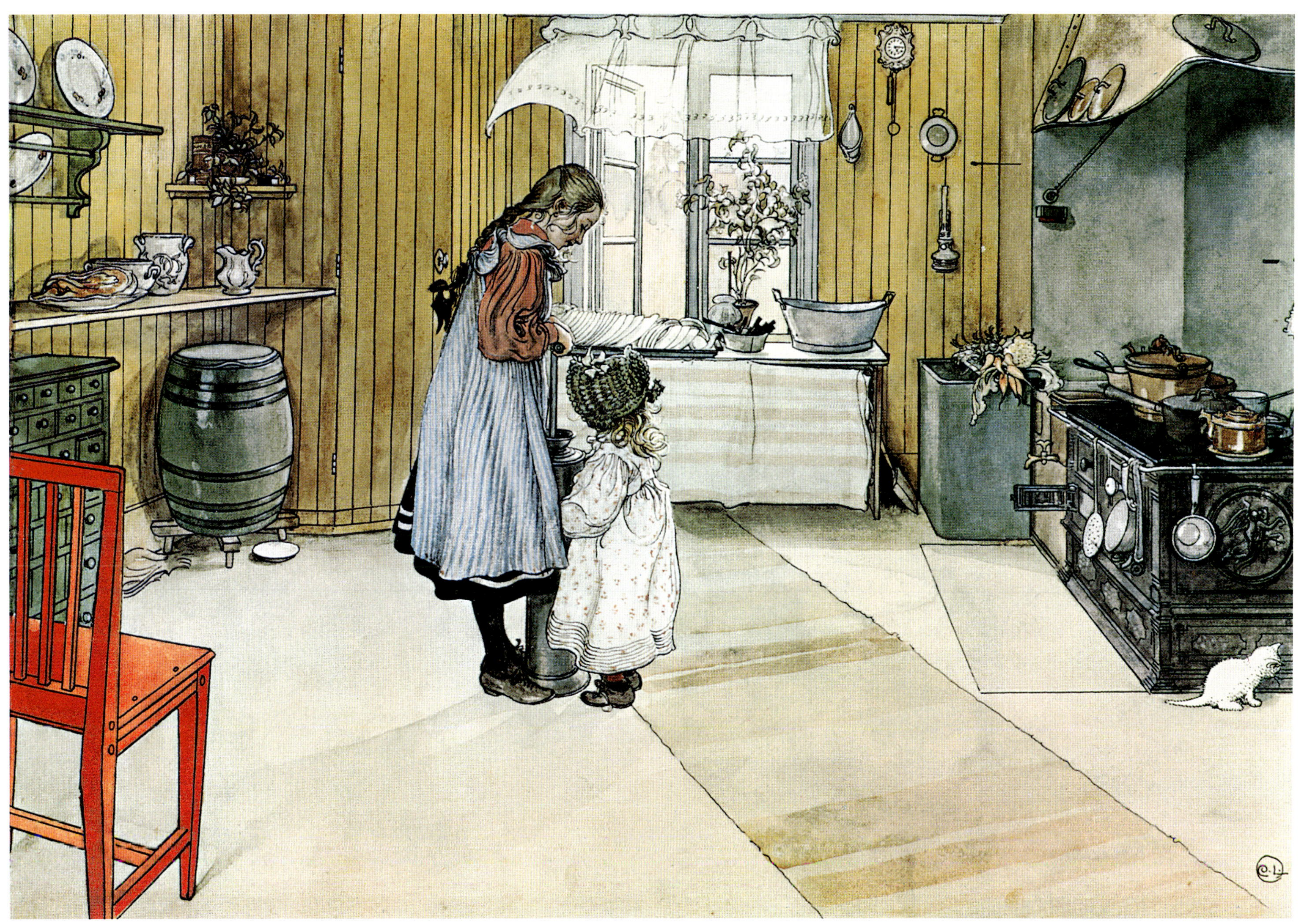

This is the bedroom where Karin slept with the three youngest girls, Brita, Lisbeth and Kersti, just a baby in this painting. Carl painted it one Sunday morning after Karin had just recovered from a serious bout of pneumonia, and the girls were moving back in. They're getting dressed in their Sunday best: chemise, bodice and pantaloons.

Unlike the kitchen, Carl made many changes to this room. The biggest one was taking out the old ceiling, to make the room more airy. He covered the wallpaper with a mix of glue and chalk, to form a white surface onto which he could paint the red bows, yellow garlands and green lilies you can see here. The painting hanging high up in the rafters is by Dalsland artist Olof Sager-Nelson.

The children used this space as a playroom, as well as for sleeping, and Carl included their wooden blocks and toys in the painting. There's also a wooden basin on the left-hand side of the room.

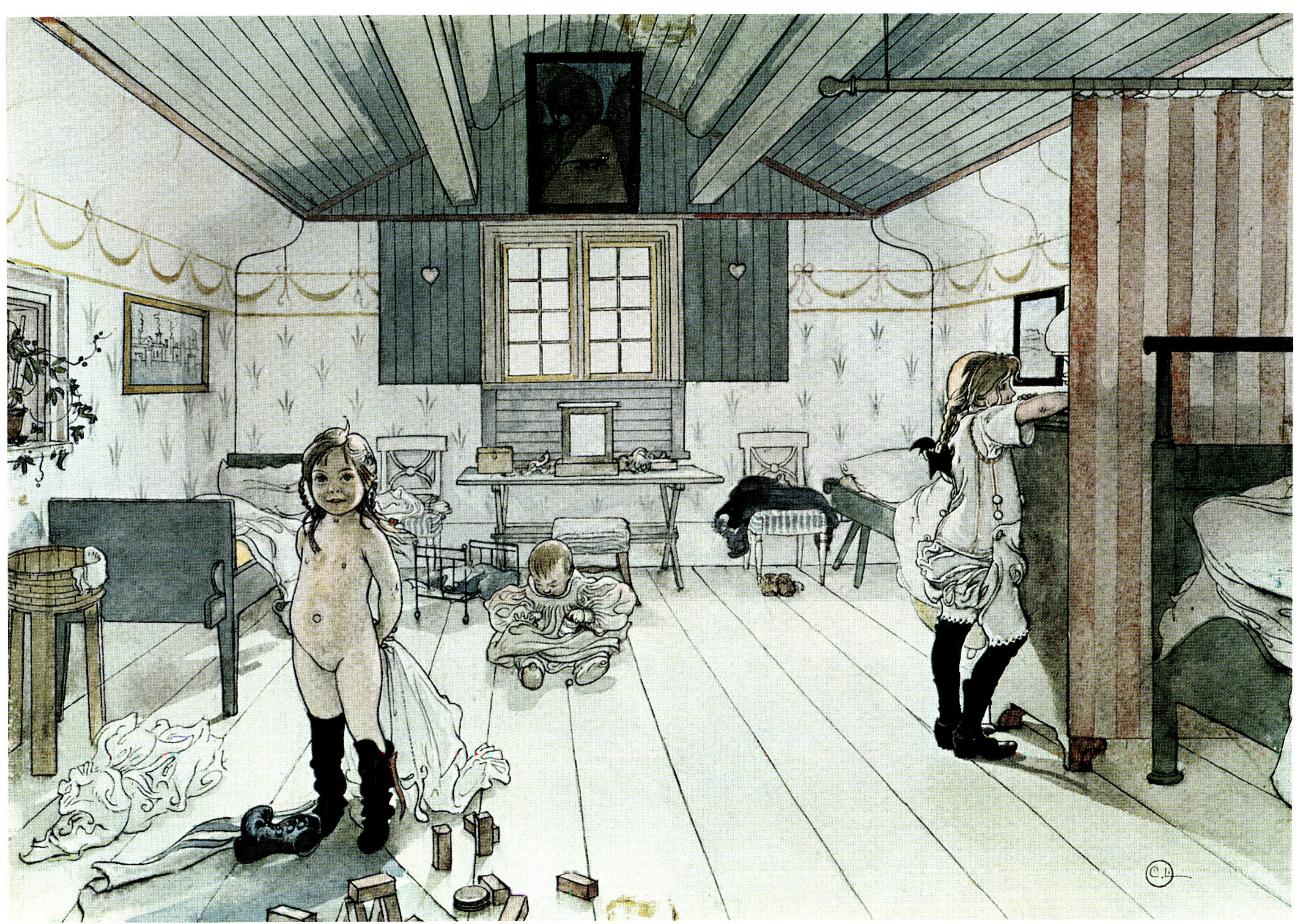

This painting is another view of Karin and the girls' room, looking in the other direction. On the left-hand side is Karin's bed; the little washbasin stand also held the chamber pot.

On the right is another tiled stove. Carl had exchanged two modern (but ugly) stoves for this one which burned day and night to keep out the cold during the Swedish winter nights.

Above the door is an inscription which reads, "For Karin, Aug. 1894." The flowers painted there include a lily, some carnations Carl had seen in southern France, and cornflowers which grew in his own meadows.

Through the door, you can see Carl's bedroom with its large central bed. There's also a hatch-window visible which looks down onto the studio.

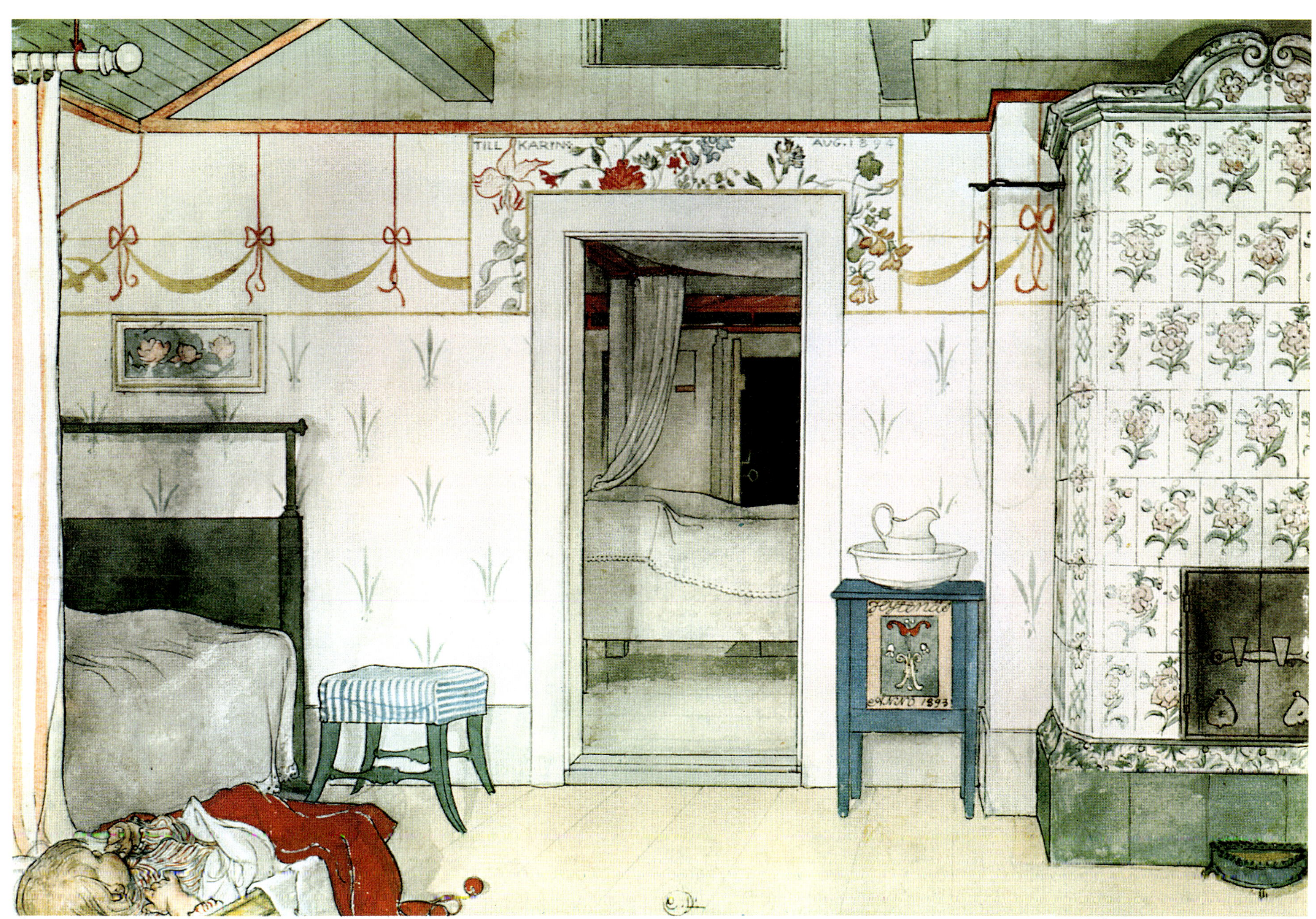
TILL KARIN
AUG. 1894
ANNO 1893

This is the only winter scene in the book, perhaps unsurprisingly. Winter days are short in Sweden, which means not much time to paint outdoors. Artist's fingers get numb, oil paints harden and watercolours freeze. In fact, Carl painted this picture from the warmth of his studio, looking at his daughter Brita through the window.

The building in the background with the wood smoke coming out of the chimney is the local bakehouse. The buildings are constructed in the traditional style, with logs from the forest fitted together, the cracks filled in with bark and moss. Carl, ever the innovator, covered his outbuildings with weather-boarding.

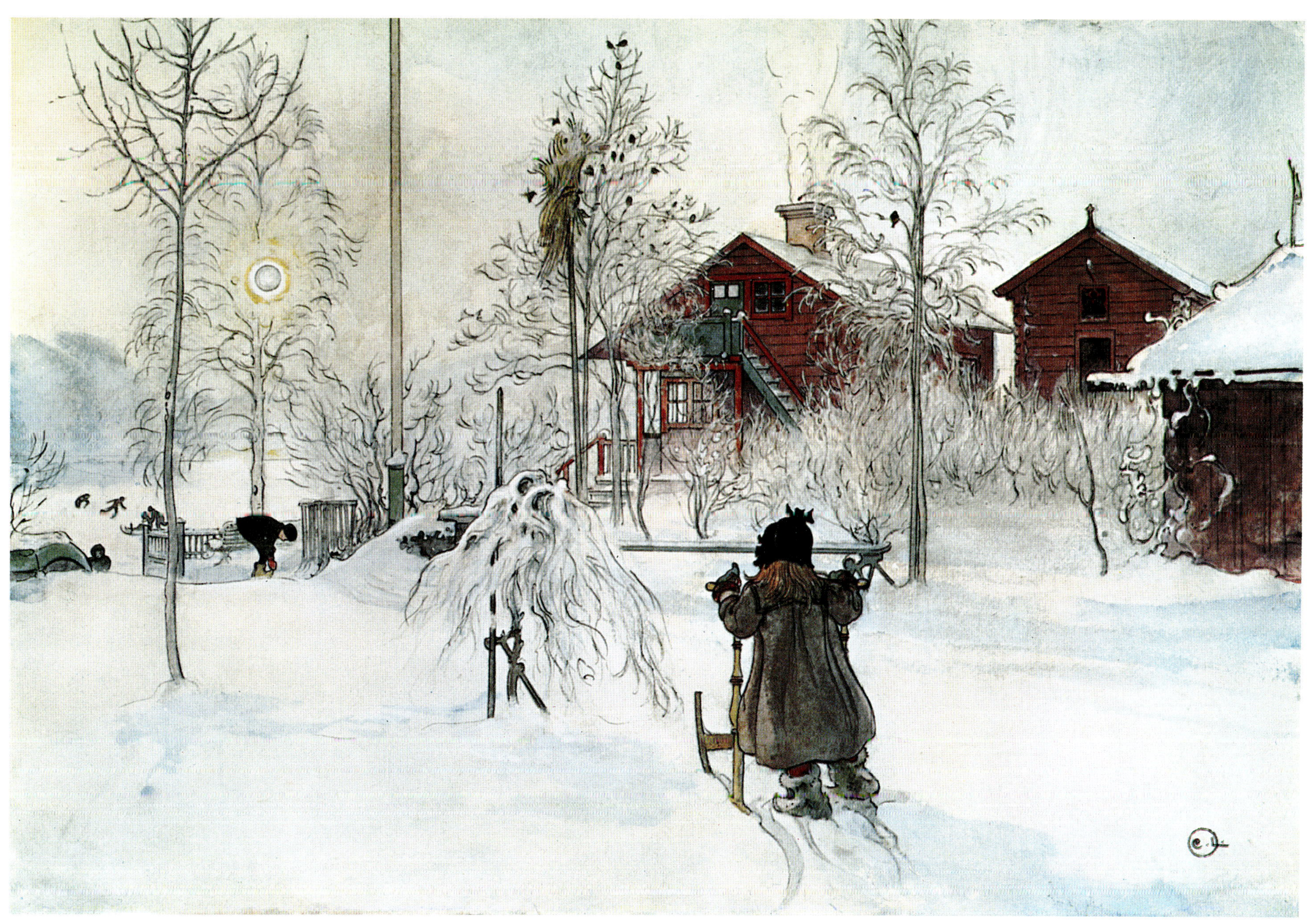

Rumble Island, in the middle of the local lake, was one of the Larsson family's favourite summer refuges. The town of Sundborn is clearly visible in the background.

The family would row across in boats and spend the day on the island. In this picture, Ulf is swimming already, and Pontus is ready to dive in; Karin sits in the shade with the baby. Carl probably painted this picture from memory.

In spring, felled logs came tumbling down the river into the lake. The first painting in this book also shows the timber rushing downstream to the local sawmill. In this painting, you can see long pieces of wood along the sides of the lake to prevent the logs from running aground.

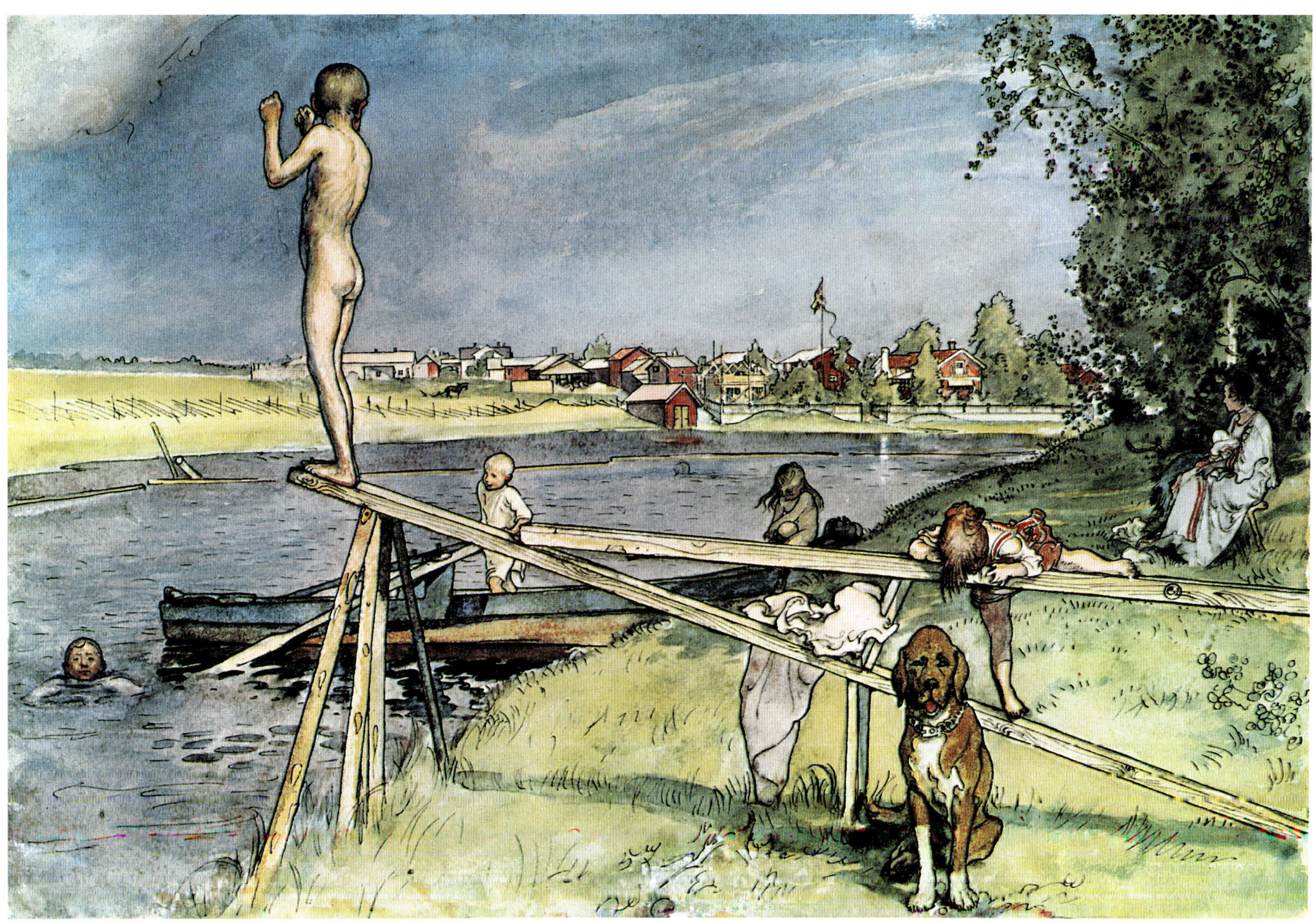

This picture was almost certainly painted on August 15th, the day the crayfishing season started. At midnight on the 15th, Carl would row out to Rumble Island and set the crayfish traps, no matter what the weather. A couple of hours in bed, then at dawn, the whole family would row out in the two boats to empty the traps.

They would fish all day, amassing dozens and dozens of crayfish, as can be seen on the plate at the front of the painting. The crayfish were boiled in the large iron washing kettle and they brewed coffee in the copper-pot. In the evening, they would enjoy a feast, wearing their best clothes.

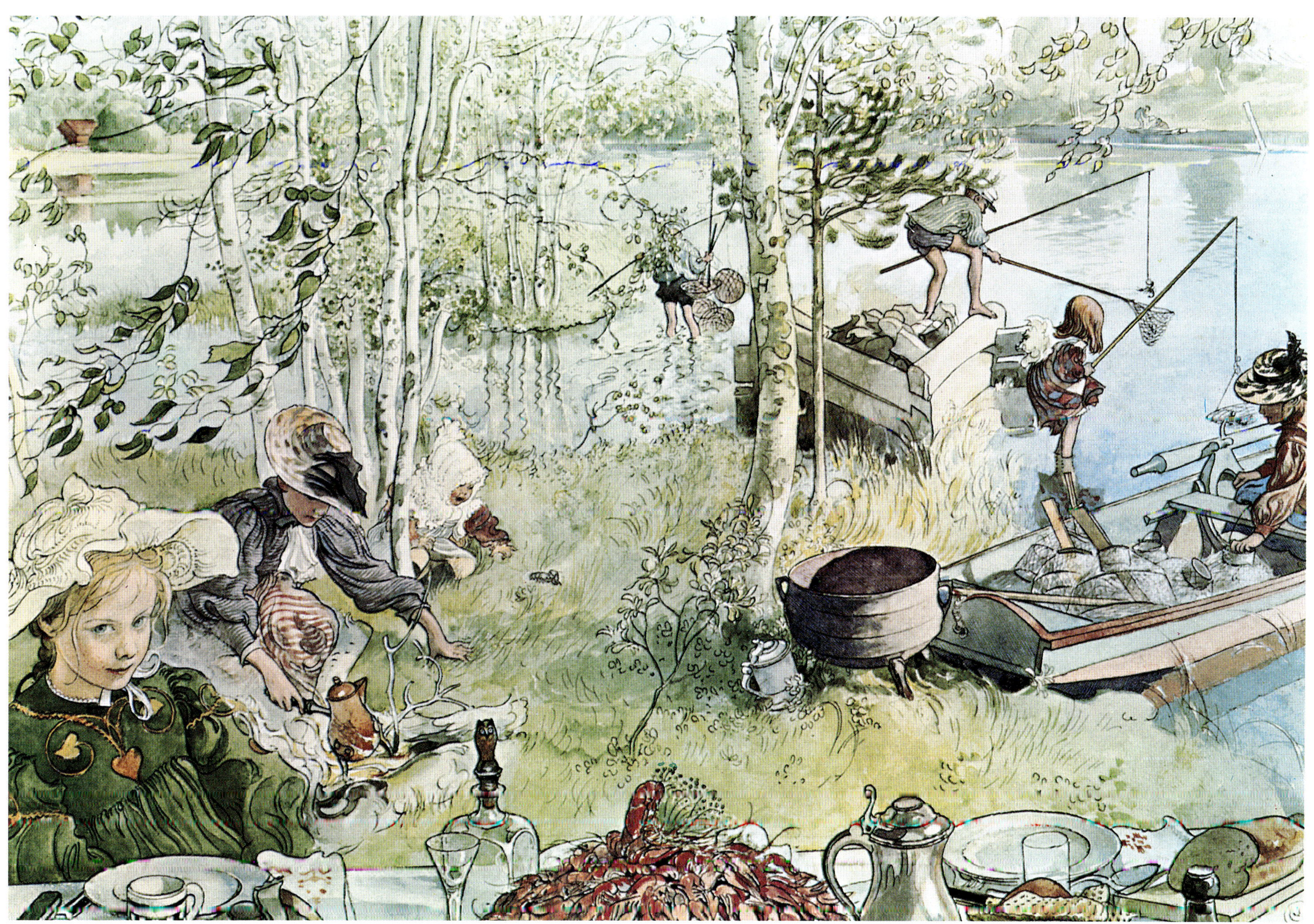

Birthdays were also an important part of the Larsson family calendar.

This painting shows the room where Anna and Emma, the maid and the cook, slept. This day was Emma's birthday and the children have raided Carl's costume and props cupboard – used to dress up models for his paintings – to put on a special show for her.

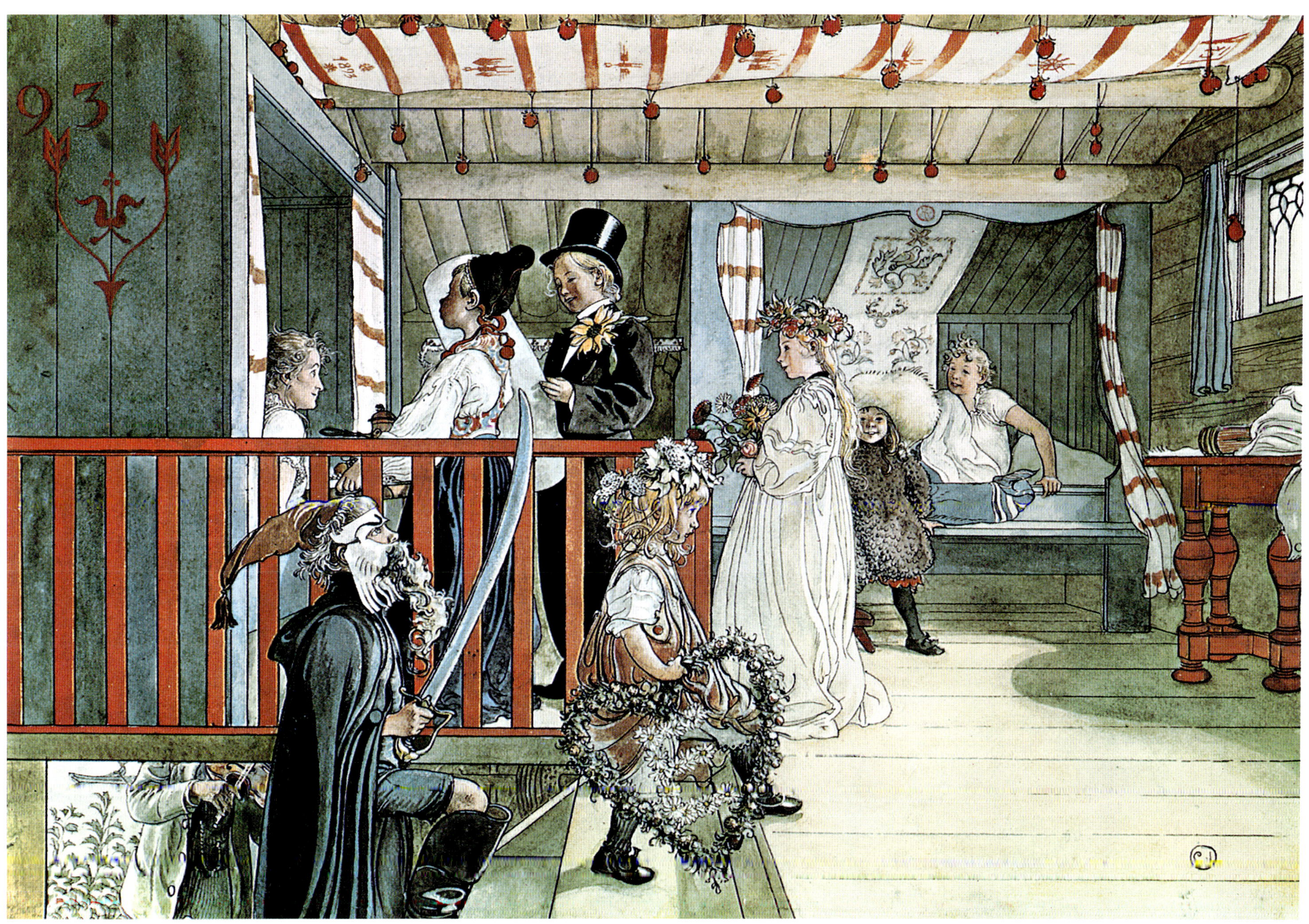

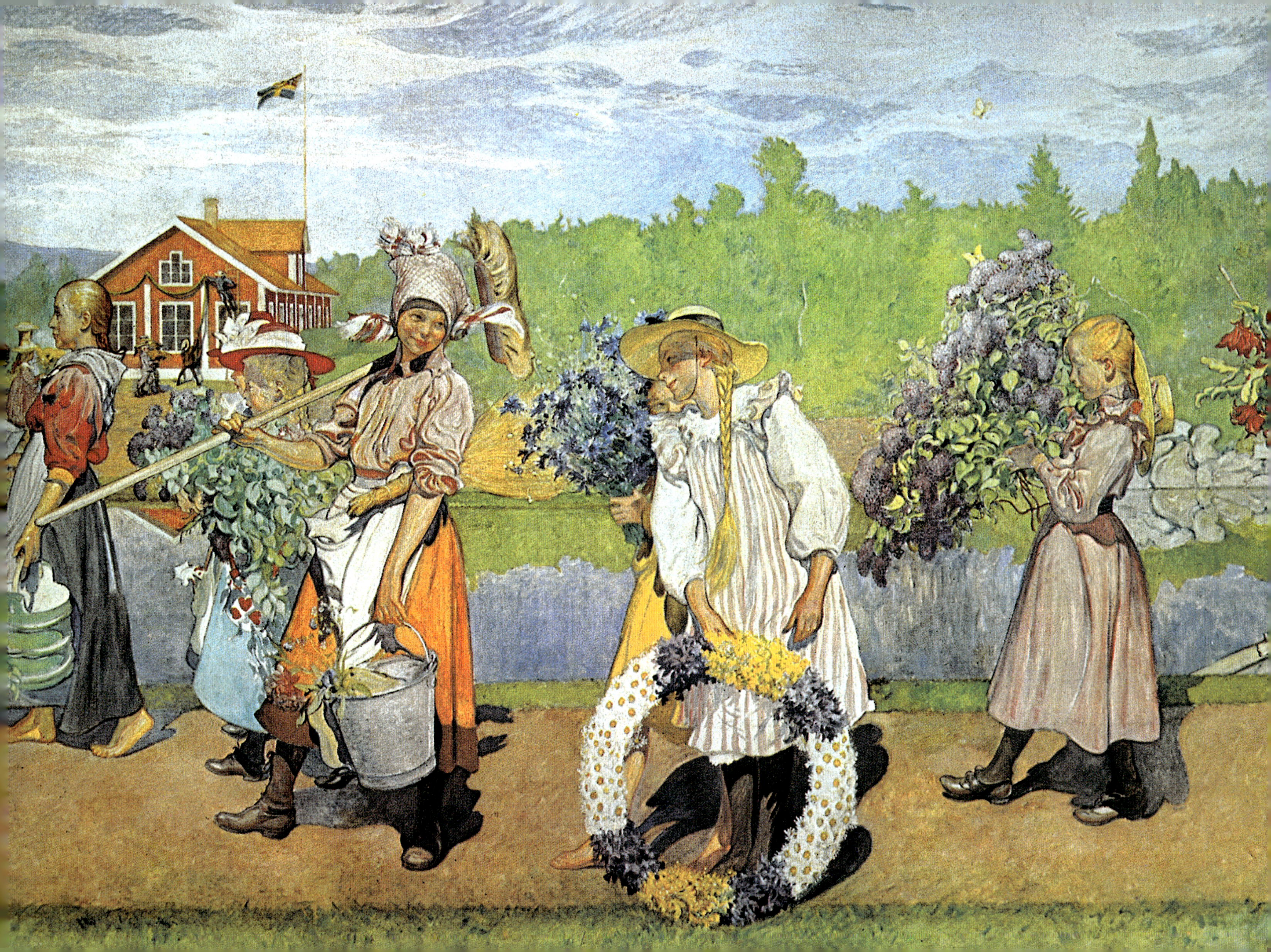

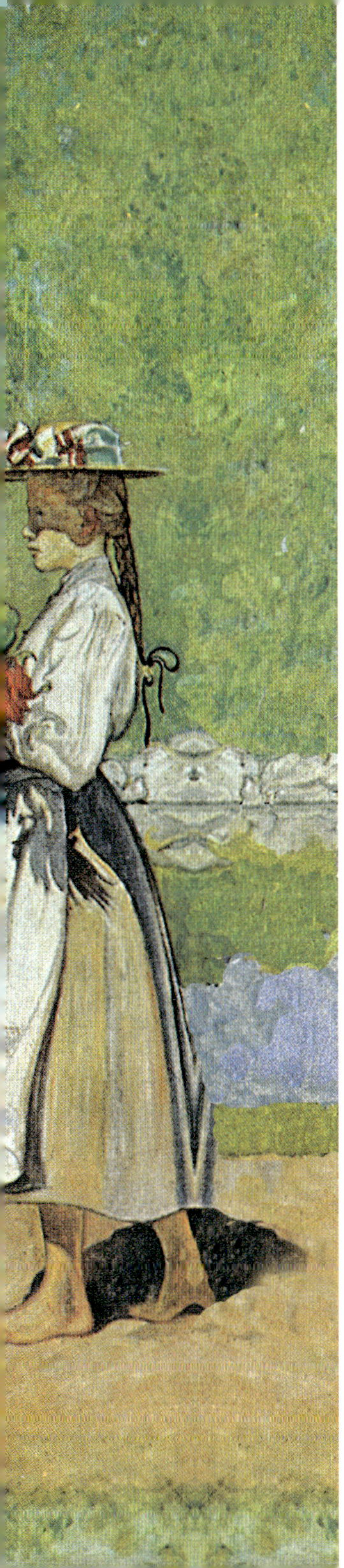

A FAMILY

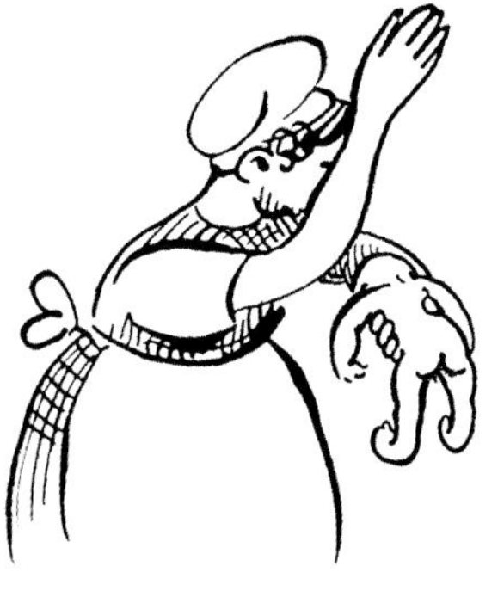

Carl Larsson was born on May 28, 1853 into a poor family in the slums of the Old Town of Stockholm. Years later he did this quick sketch (see left) of his birth as he imagined it.

The family lived in a derelict two-room apartment, and Carl was frequently ill. His difficult childhood was tempered, however, by adults who encouraged his artistic skills: a seamstress who lived next door, who had fashion plates pinned to her walls; Corporal Ärtman (see right) who would bring him stubs of used pencils and paper for drawing; and his teachers at the free school for poor children who supported his painting.

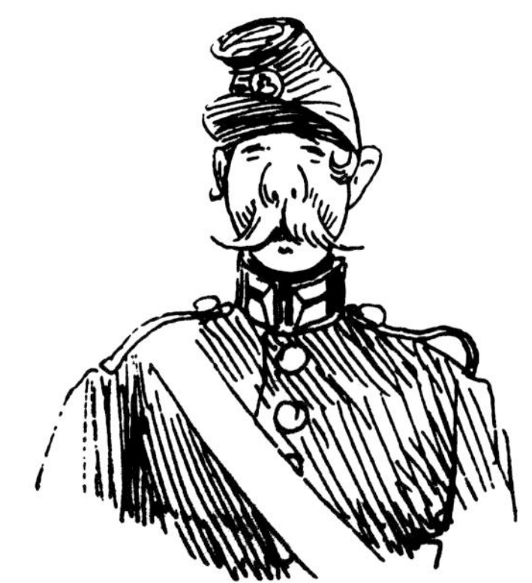

At the age of thirteen, he was accepted to the preparatory school of the Academy of Fine Arts, and then to the Academy itself. This would prove to be his way out of desperate poverty, and he was determined that his own children would grow up in a safer, happier environment than he had.

The three paintings opposite are an introduction to some of Carl's family: on the left are Ulf and Pontus, playing at soldiers; Carl himself with their fifth child, Brita, on his shoulders; and on the right, Carl's wife, Karin, with Kersti, their youngest daughter.

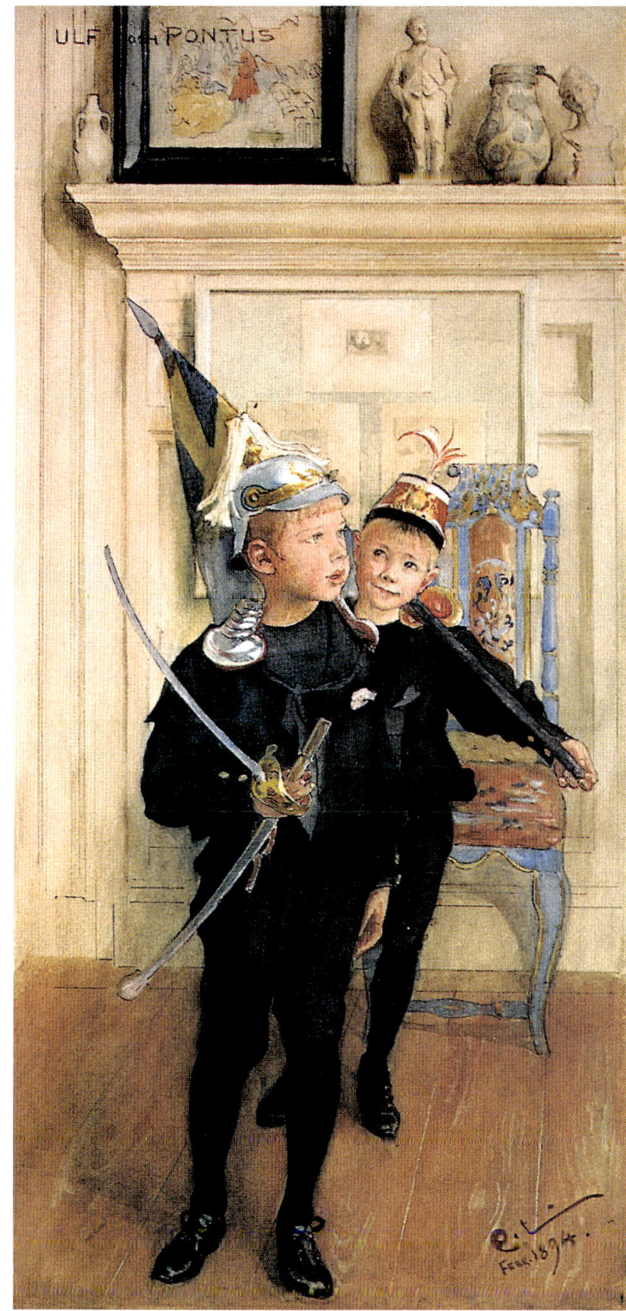

ULF och PONTUS
C L
1894

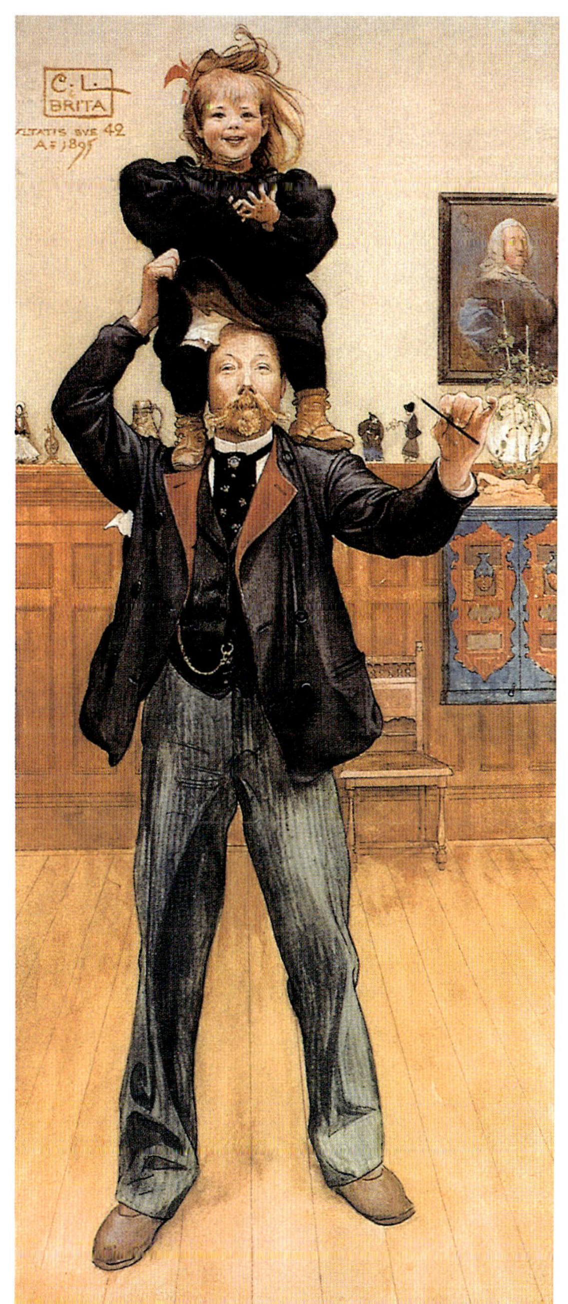

C. L.
BRITA
ÆTATIS SVÆ 42
AÃ 1895

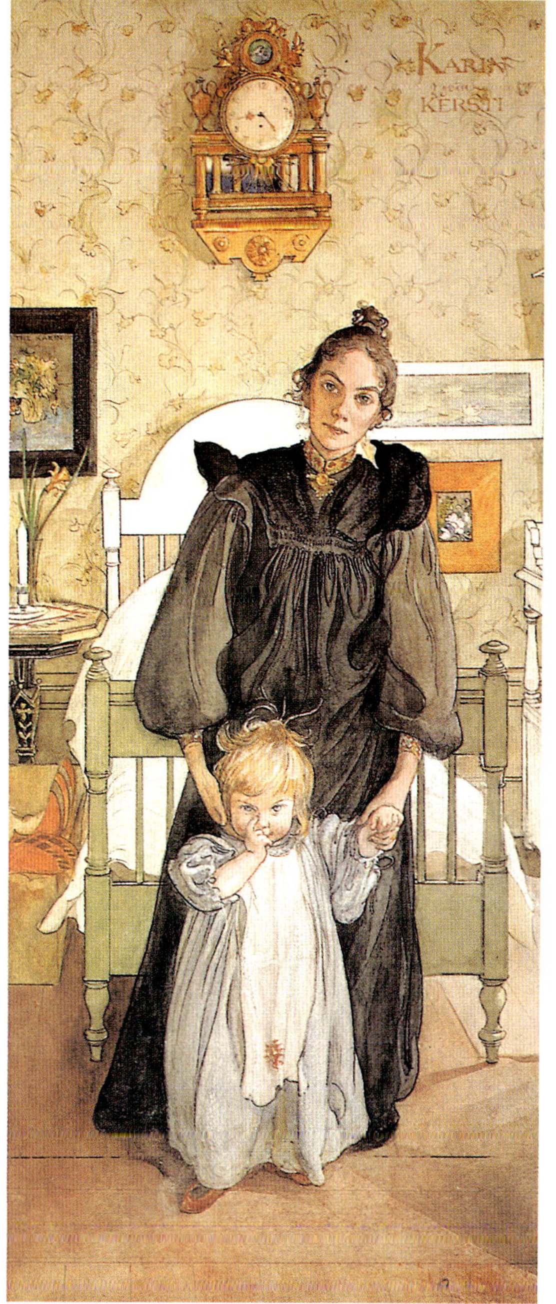

KARIN
och
KERSTI

As a young artist, Carl moved to Grez, a small French village outside Paris, where he lived in an artists' community. It was here that he met Karin, also an artist, and they got married in 1883. Suzanne, their first child, was born in 1884. Carl wrote, "Now, I am the happiest man in the world. I turn cartwheels and somersaults!"

These two paintings of Karin and Suzanne in Grez were done over the Christmas of 1884. In *A Studio Idyll,* on the left, Karin sits in a wicker chair with the sleepy baby. Most of Carl's later paintings of his home and family were watercolours, but here he used pastels on grey, textured paper. First he drew in the dark areas of the picture, then finished with the touches of light on Karin's collar, cheek and chin, and on Suzanne's forehead. *Little Suzanne* on the right, which was painted in oils, started life as a picture of just the room – Suzanne and Karin were added in later.

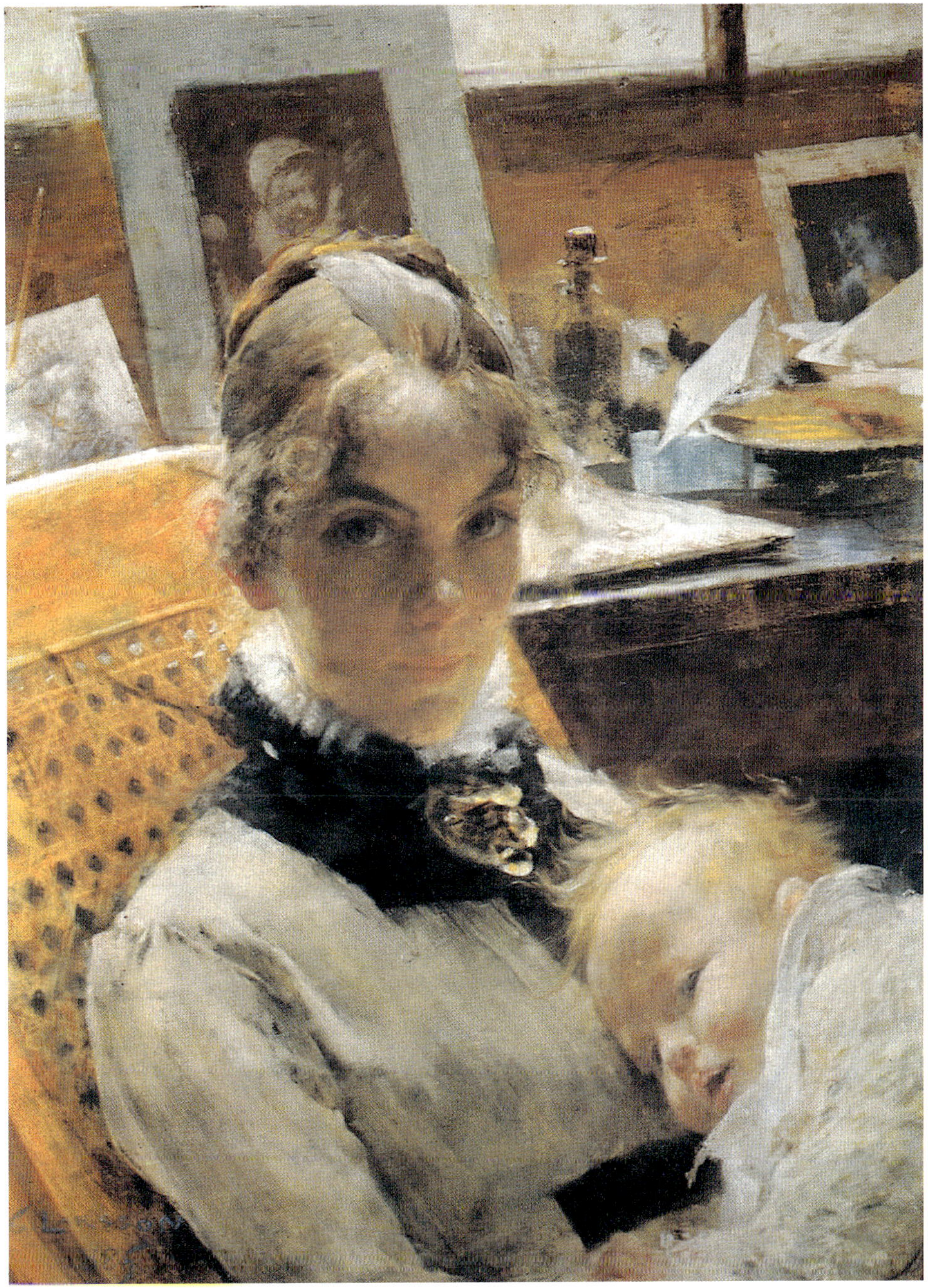

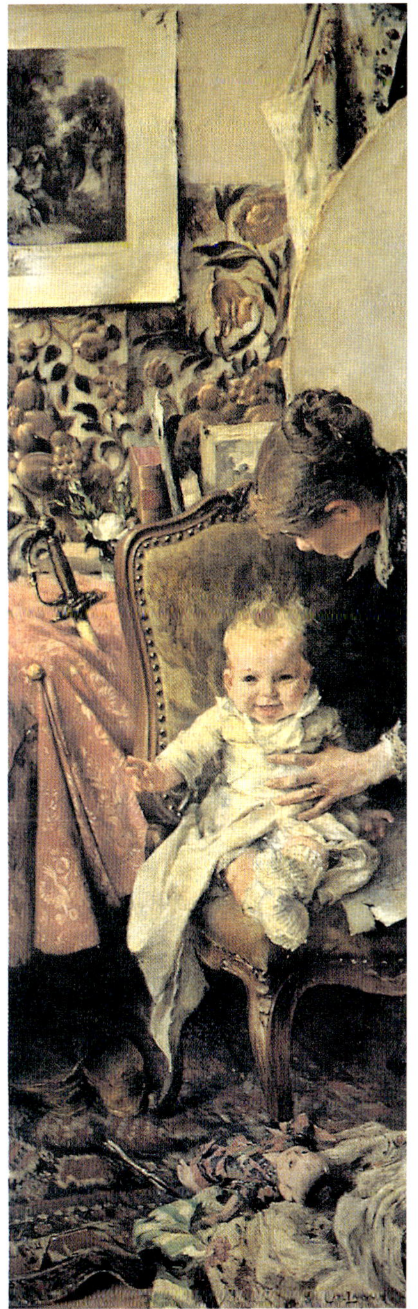

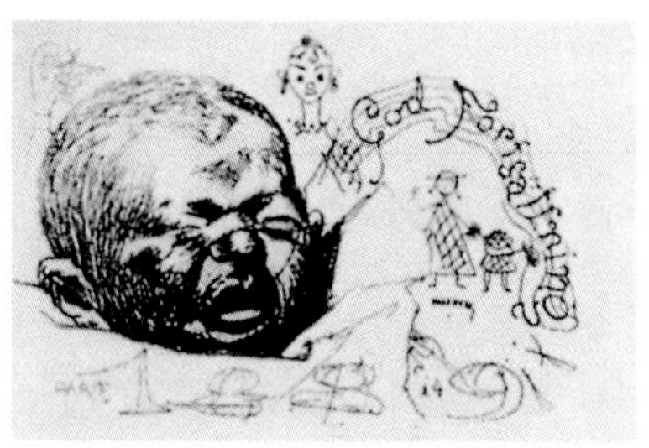

Being penniless artists was less easy now that they had a child, and in 1885 the Larssons returned to Stockholm. The three of them lived in a tiny apartment, and Carl worked as a newspaper and book illustrator, as well as teaching art. In 1886, they moved to Gothenburg where Carl taught at Valand School of Fine Art, and their eldest son, Ulf, was born. A year later they were back in France and a second son, Pontus, was born.

Carl was busy with work – in particular, he was working on sketches for a mural for the National Museum of Stockholm – but he made time to do some quick drawings of his growing family. This painting, *Pontus on the Floor,* which shows their youngest child sitting on one of Karin's rag rugs, was completed in oils.

On the left is an etching of the new-born Pontus that Carl created for a New Year's greeting card. First, he drew the picture onto a copper plate covered with beeswax and soot. The copper was then treated with acid to produce an engraved plate which could be used in a printing machine.

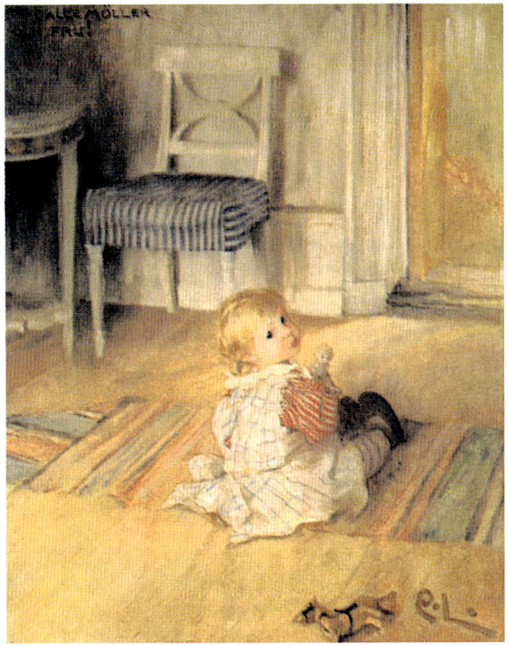
ALLE MÖLLER
FRU!

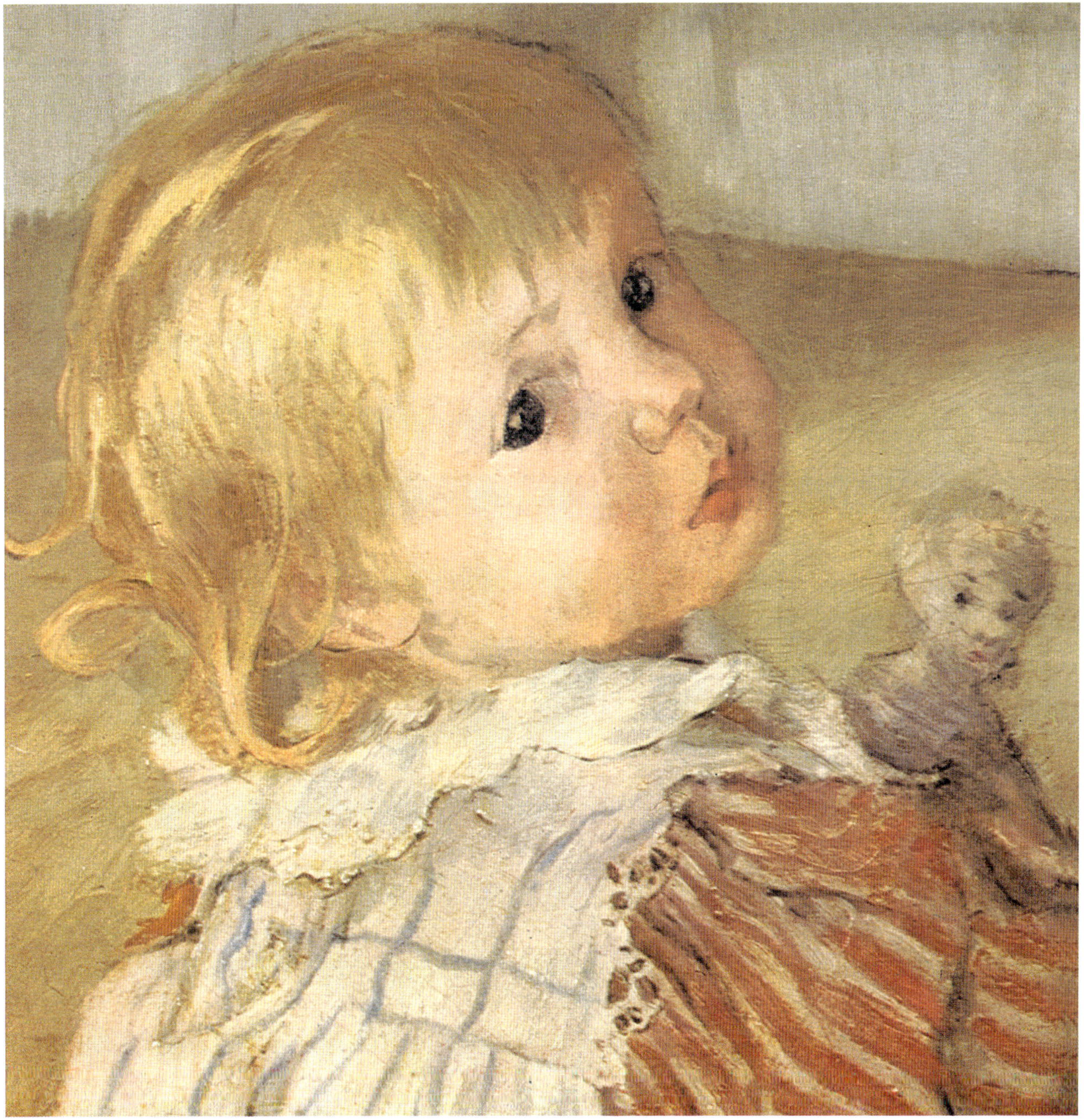

In 1888, the Larssons moved back to Sweden for the final time, to a cottage in Sundborn which had been given to them by Karin's father. Lisbeth was born in 1891, followed by Brita in 1893. The painting opposite shows Karin breastfeeding two-week-old Brita during a holiday on the west coast of Sweden in a fisherman's cottage. The sun is shining on the rocks outside, but indoors the room and furnishings are dark, quite different from the light, bright colours of their Sundborn home.

During the early years at Sundborn, Karin supervised various extensions to the cottage, created its garden and furnishings, and looked after their family, while Carl worked on different artistic projects. He painted a mural, *The History of Women*, for a girls' school in Gothenburg, and for two years worked on the illustrations for a book by Elias Sehlstedt called *Songs and Ditties*, from which this sketch of a cow is taken.

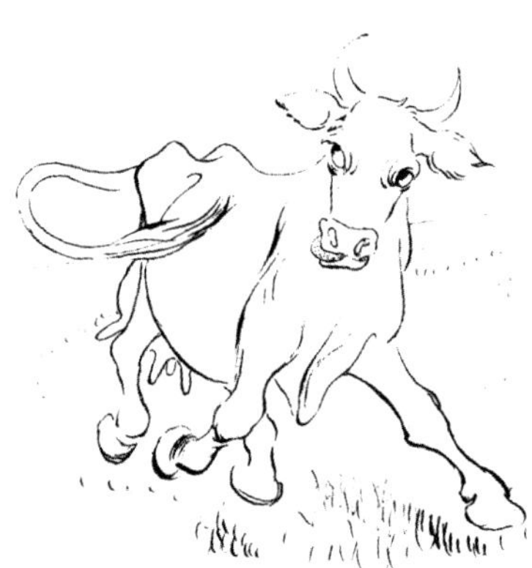

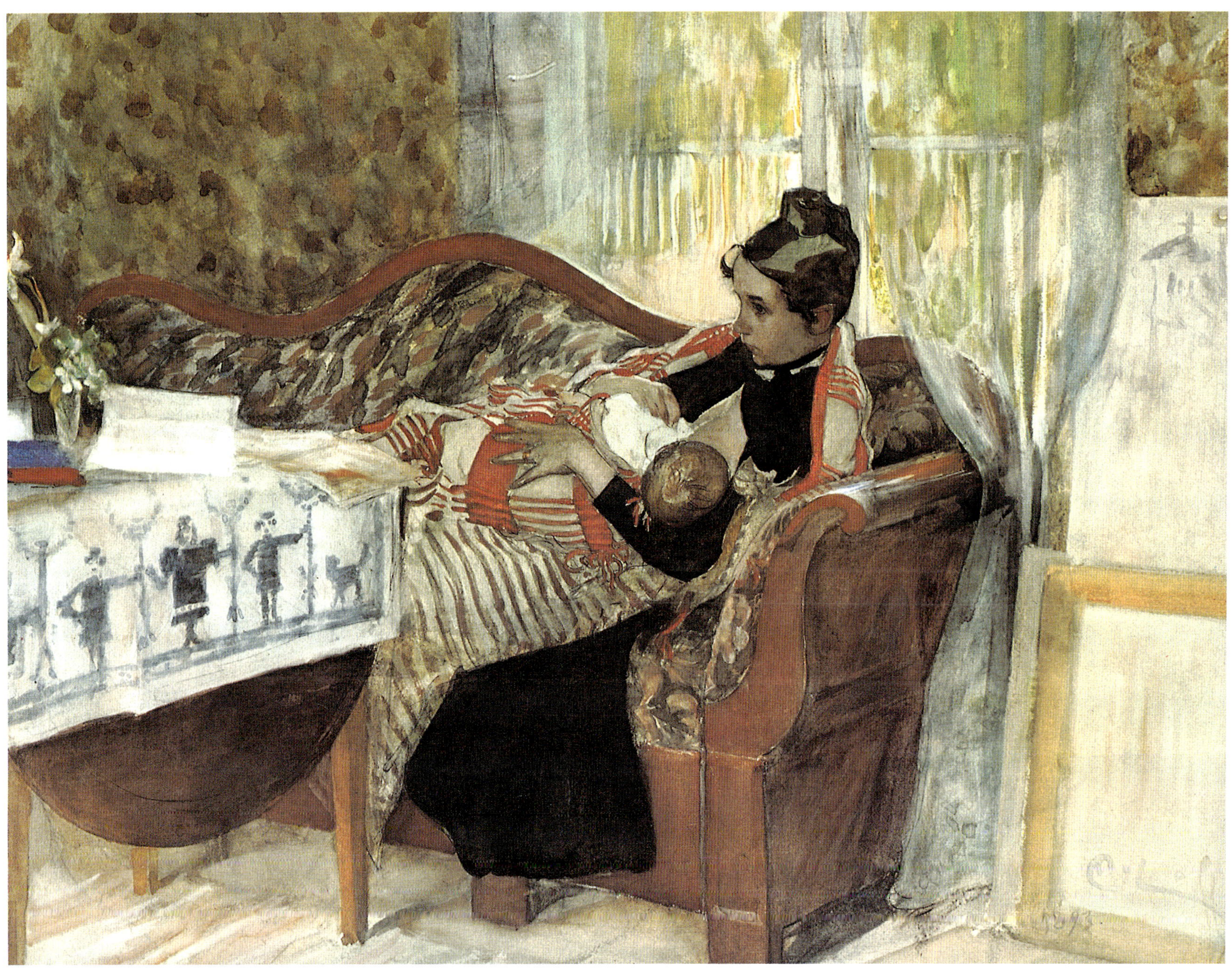

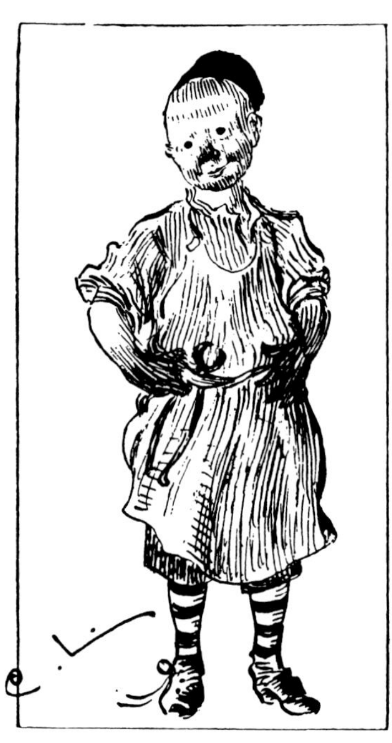

Carl's portraits of his children were spotted by an art dealer, and soon he began to receive more commissions. The left-hand painting is Lisbeth in 1894, in red stockings, a red dress, a red apron and carrying her red doll. "Lisbeth, the little rascal," wrote Carl, "is like a little troll sparkling in the sunshine. There is brightness and glitter around her, and bubbling and tinkling laughter. There is giggling, and there is no sorrow wherever she goes."

The same year saw him paint the portrait on the right of ten-year-old Suzanne. In contrast to Lisbeth, she looks uneasy, standing on a stool and fiddling with her black dress. Carl often had his children pose as models for his large commissioned paintings and murals, frequently wearing historical costumes researched, designed and made by Karin.

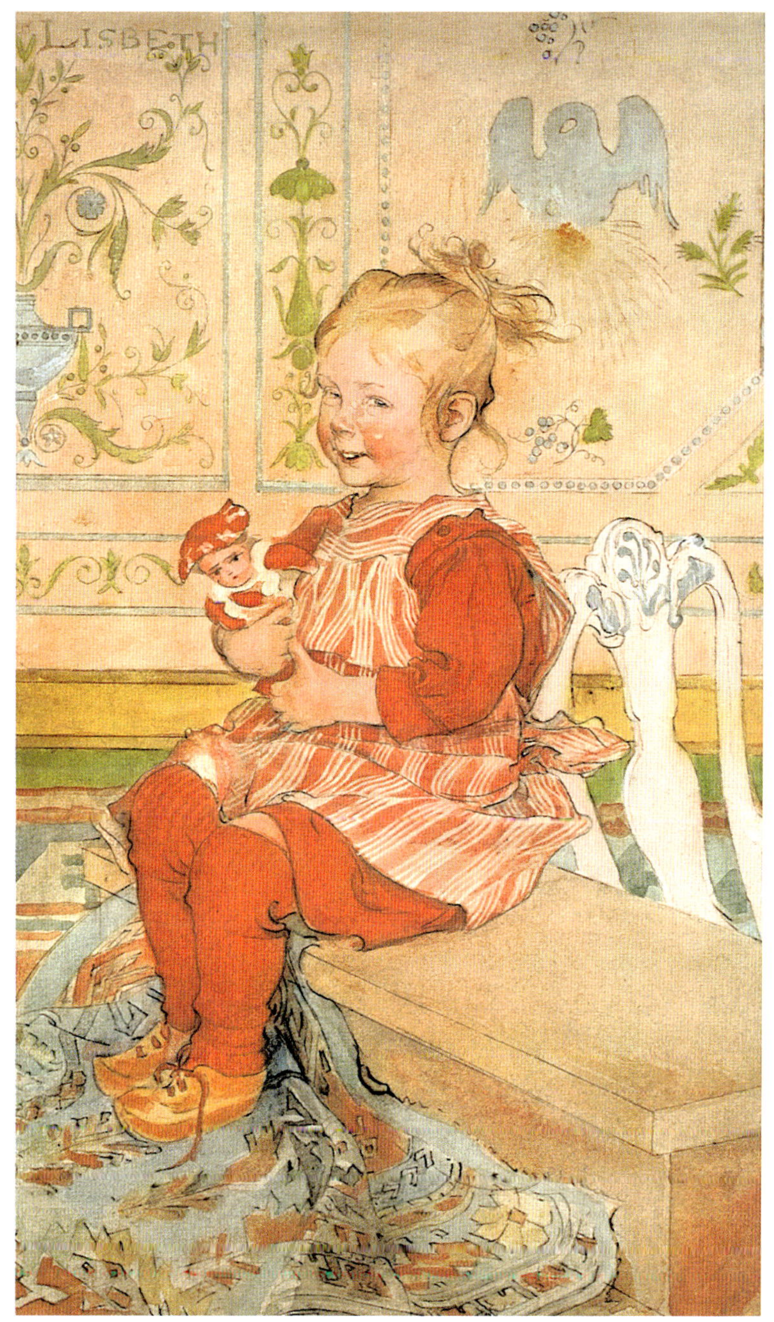
LISBETH

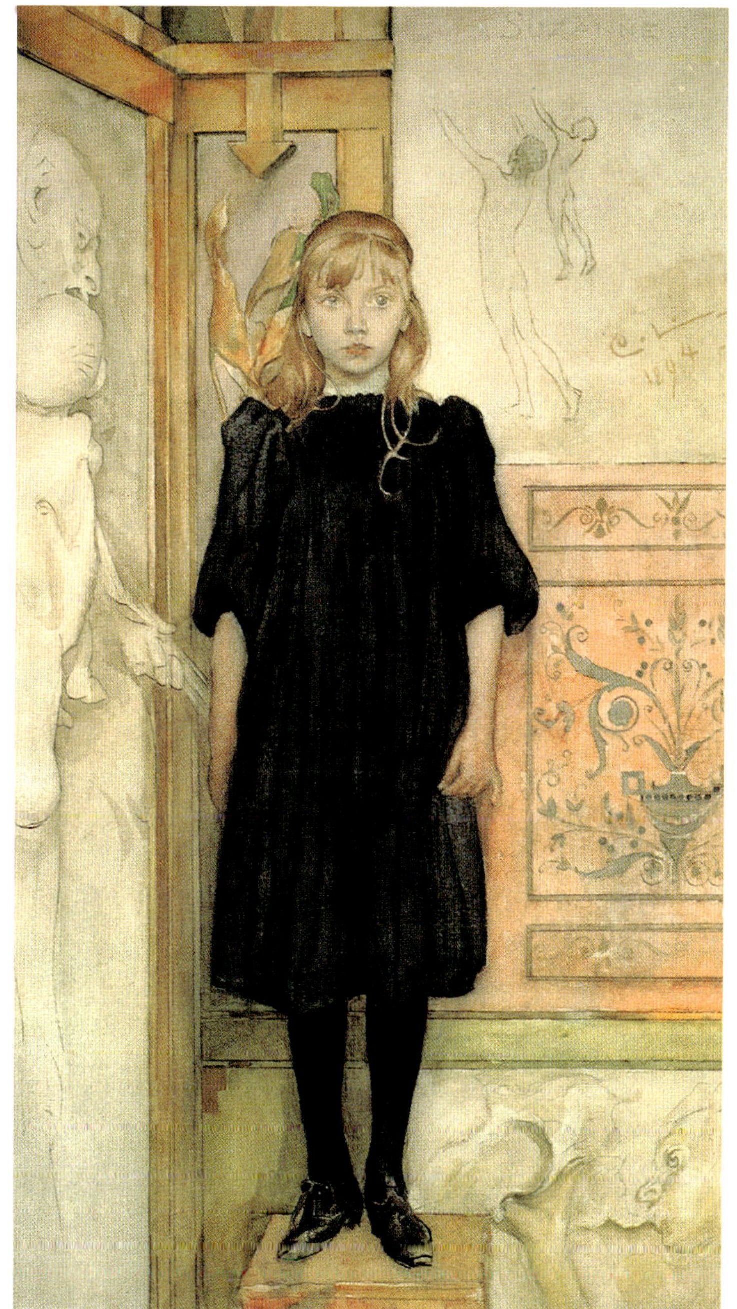
SUZANNE
1894

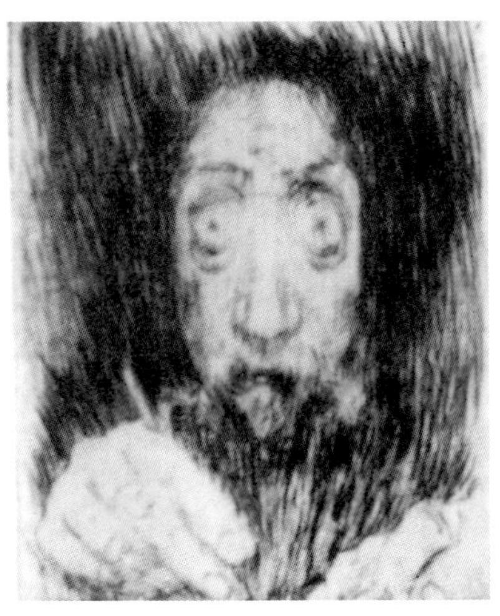

In the summer of 1894, it rained for six weeks without stopping. Carl was unable to paint outdoors, so on Karin's suggestion, he started painting scenes of the inside of their home. That autumn, the paintings were exhibited in Stockholm to much acclaim, and five years later they were published in the book entitled *A Home*. The book seemed to depict a household free from worry; so serene were its paintings that some soldiers took a copy of the book with them into the trenches of the First World War, as relief from what was happening around them.

Larsson family life was not always idyllic, of course. Carl called this haunted-looking self-portrait "the writer's ghost".

Carl's success encouraged him to keep painting his home and family. This picture is of Lisbeth fishing off a rowboat jetty. The children frequently caught pike and perch in the Sundborn river, shown here on a calm day with the birch trees reflected mirror-like in the still water.

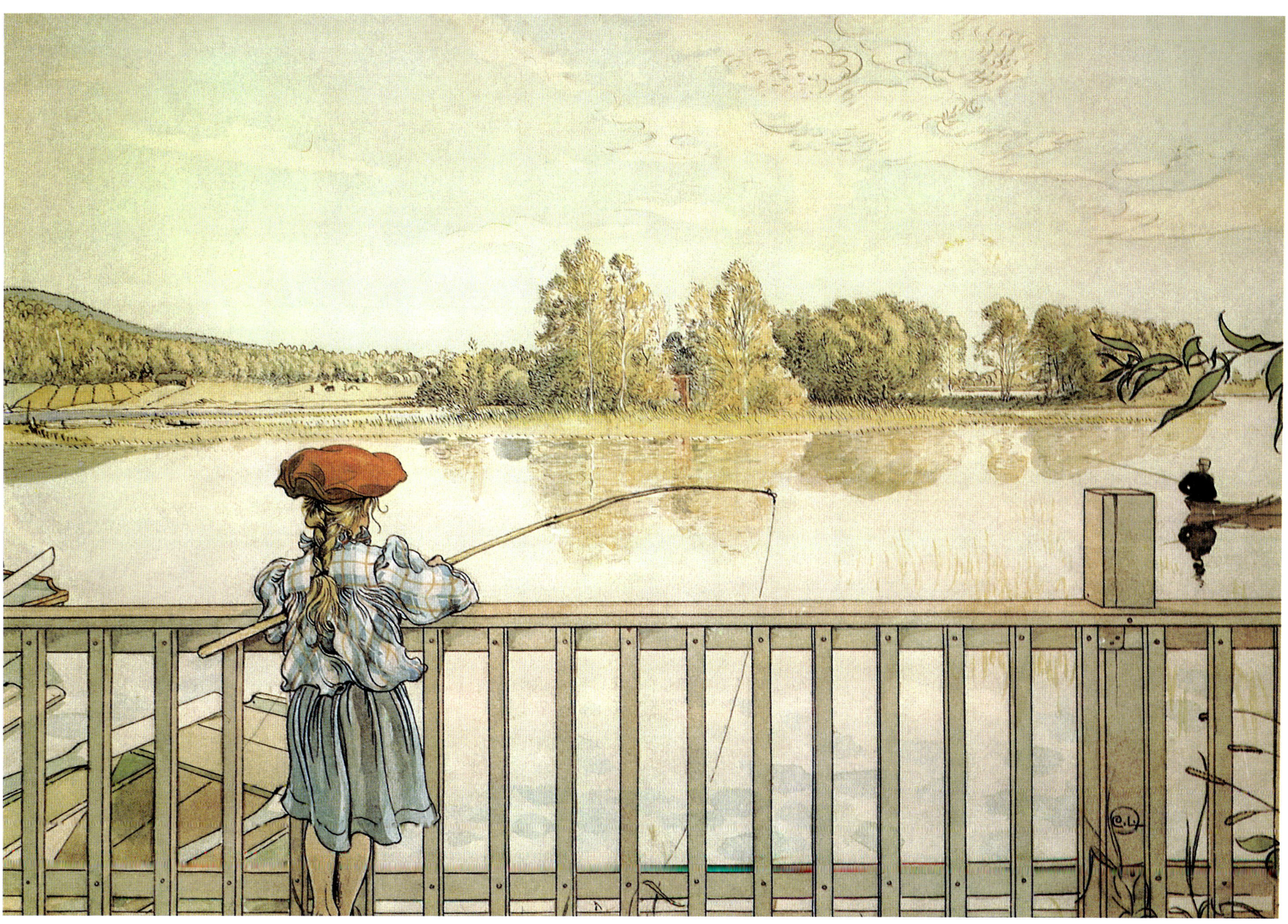

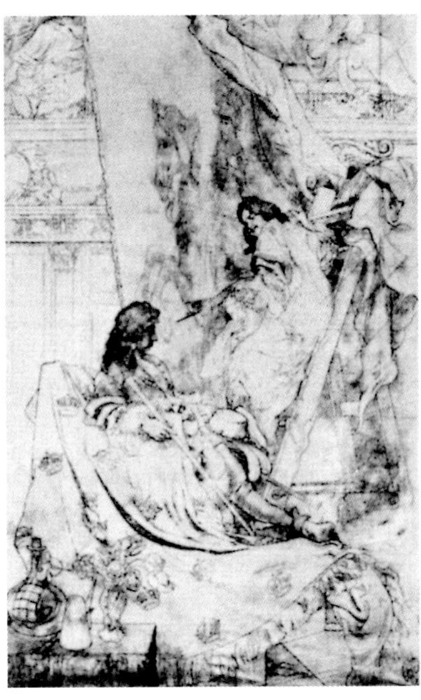

The year 1897 was memorable for the Larsson family. Carl and Karin's sixth child, Kersti, had recently been born. Carl finally finished – and was paid for – the mural paintings in the National Museum in Stockholm. The Larssons used the money to buy two nearby farms: Spadarvet and Kartbacken.

Carl's parents went to live at Kartbacken, while Johan and Johanna, who ran the farm, stayed on at Spadarvet, which was just five minutes' walk from the Larsson's house. This painting is of Brita standing on the path at Spadarvet a few years later, eating bread and jam from the farm kitchen. Carl would have done a quick pencil sketch, put in the outline with India ink, and then painted in the colours afterwards.

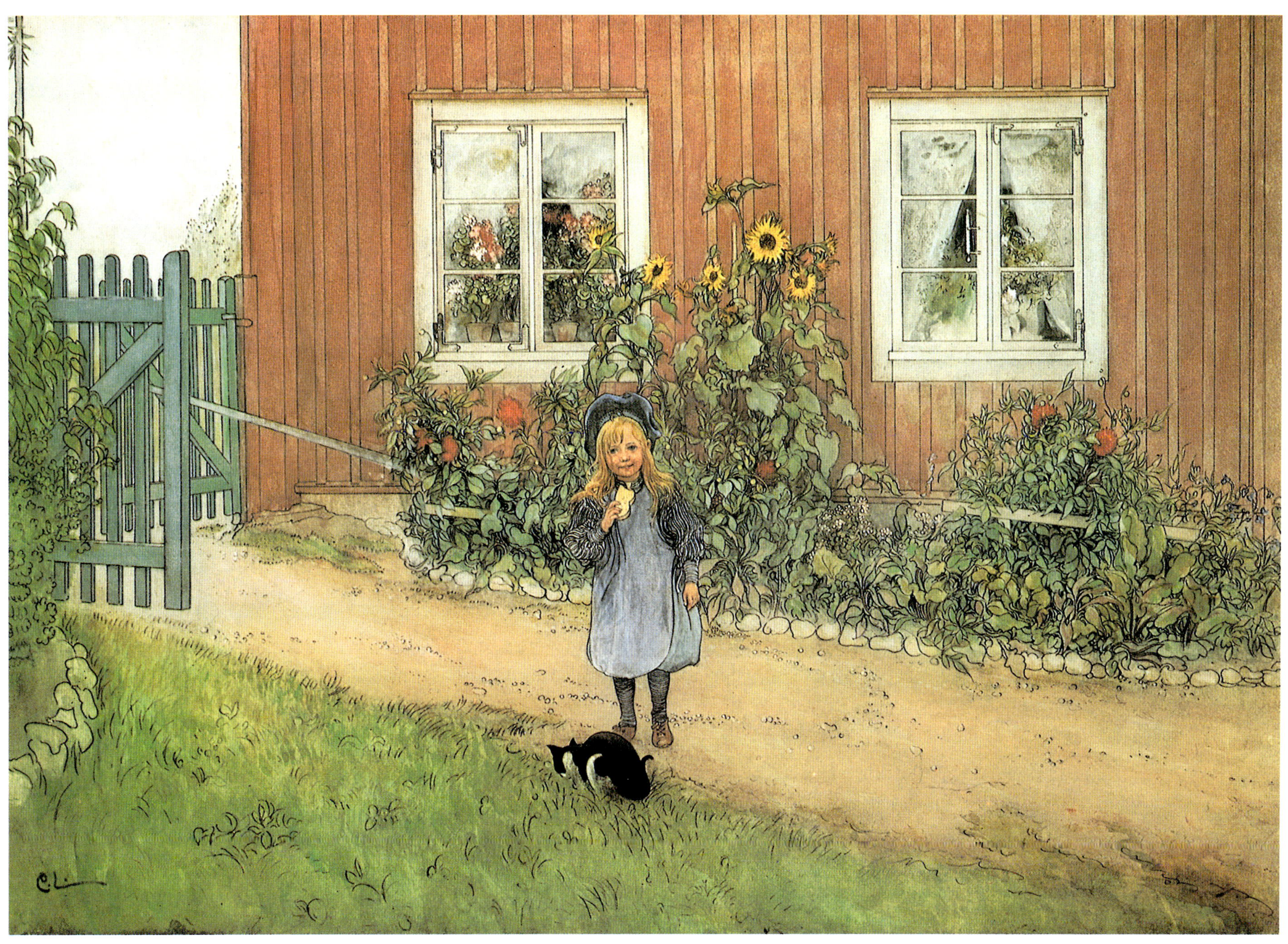

In 1900, the final Larsson child was born: Esbjörn. The painting on the right shows him sitting on Karin's lap. Carl painted this work quickly, using lots of water in the paint, so that the baby would look delicately translucent. The sketch below is also of Esbjörn, suffering from mumps.

The painting on the left is of the Larsson's dining room, at the end of supper. Karin stands with Esbjörn in the shadowed corner, ready to say goodnight. The other children are also half-seen, and the focus is on the table itself: the jugs, bowls, plates, half-finished rolls, flowers and the glowing oil lamp.

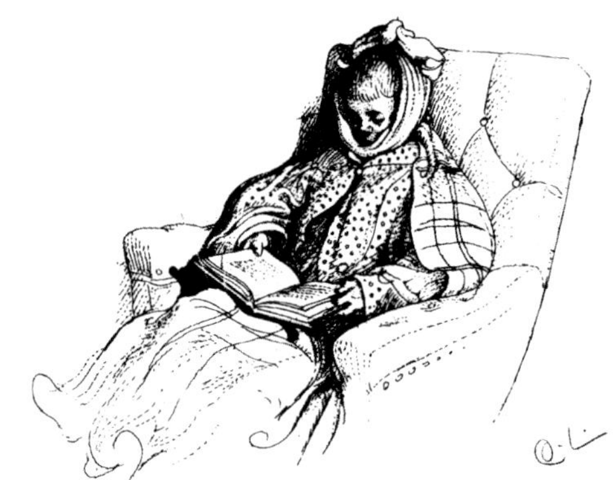

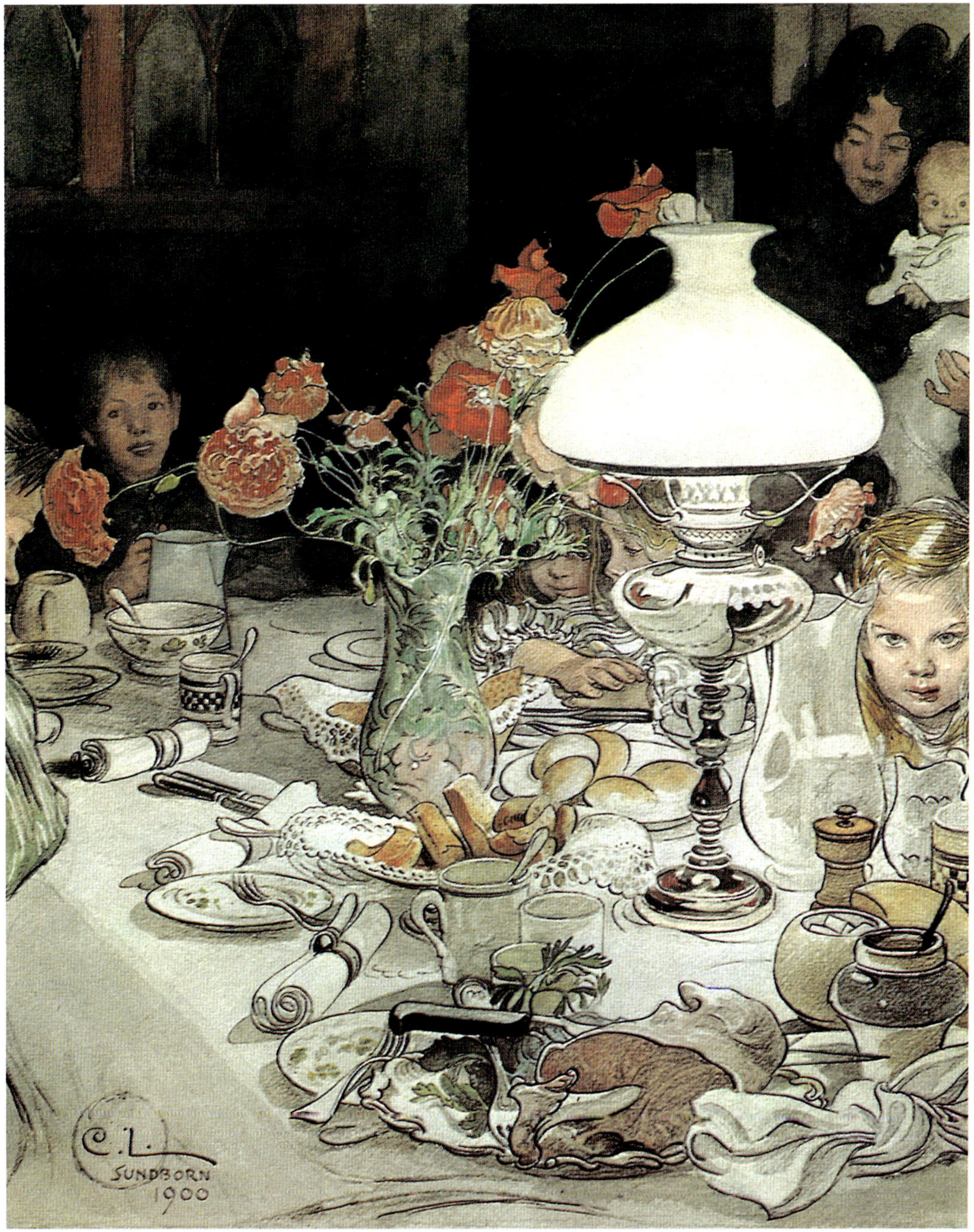

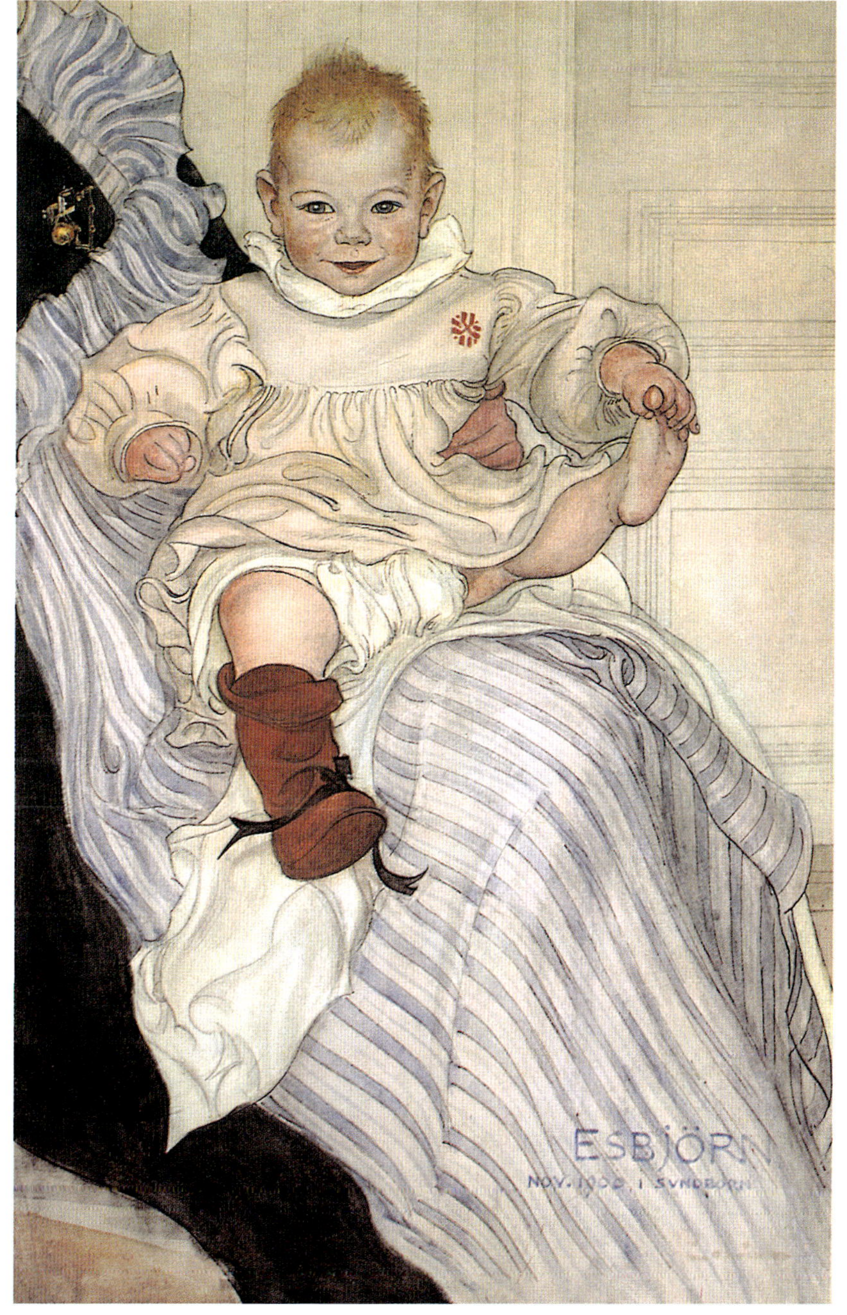

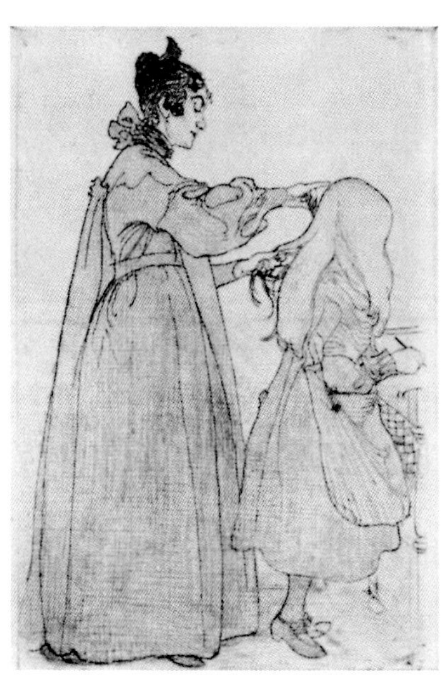

This painting from the following year, called *Getting Ready For A Game,* shows the same dining room, the same table, and the same oil lamp. But instead of the late summer evening of the painting on the previous page, this scene shows a dark winter night, with a storm raging outside. Carl wrote, "It is terrible outdoors. The wind is whistling at the corners of the house, and the snow isn't snow, it is needles stabbing your eyes. And while you are crying, hobgoblins are whipping your back with canes. Oh, to get indoors and play a game of cards!"

Brita and Kersti watch Carl working from one end of the table, while Karin prepares drinks – she's reaching for a bottle of Benedictine – for imminent guests. Above the door through to the candle-lit room, where the adults will later play cards, Carl has painted "Guds Fred", meaning "God's Peace."

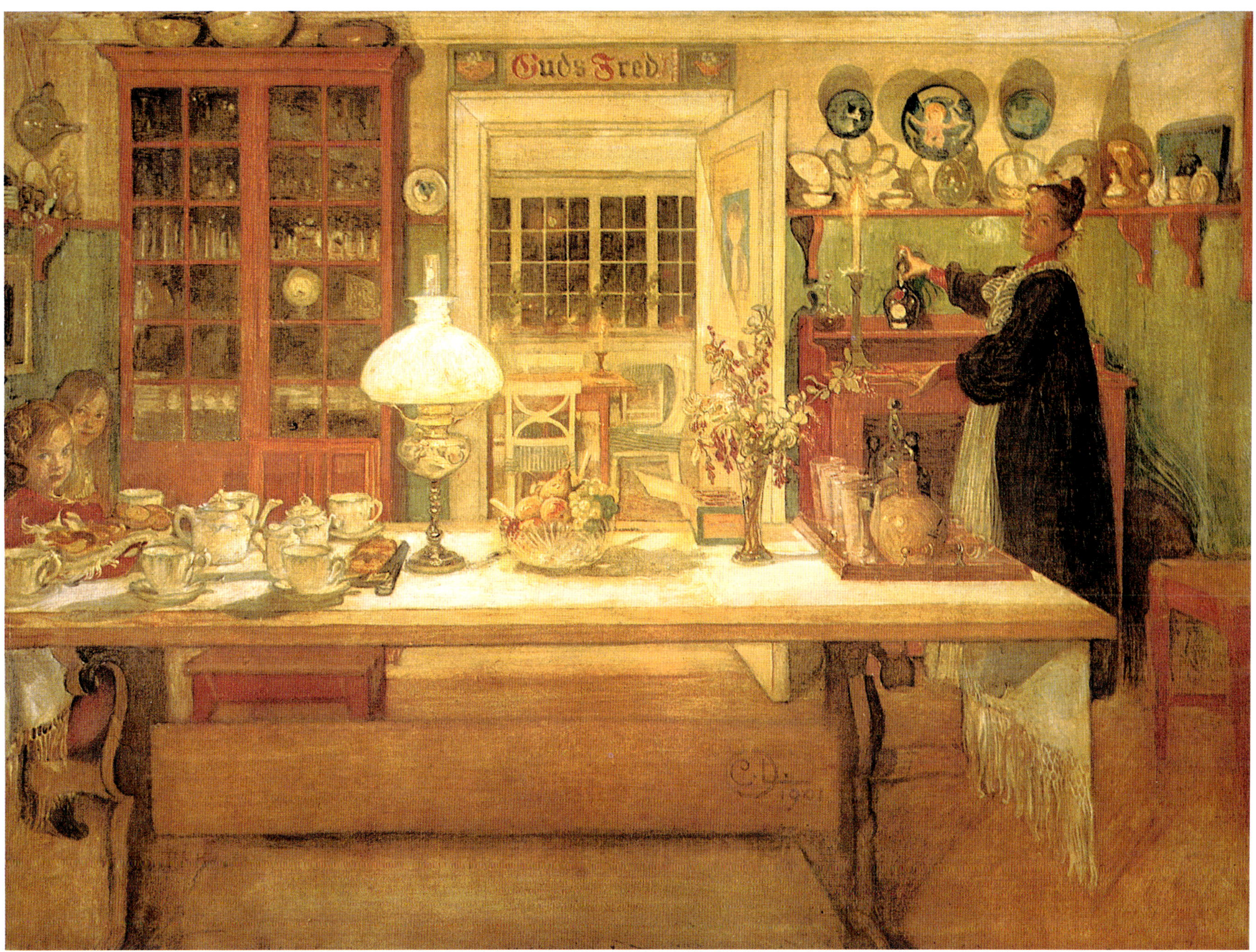

Guds Fred

The smell of fresh paint was familiar in the Larsson house. In the picture on the left, Suzanne is painting a coloured border around the top of the walls, and has paused to study her work. At the same time, two men are painting the outside of the house — one only visible by his feet. Light pours into the room, catching Suzanne's braid and the folds of her apron.

In contrast, the hunched figure in the painting on the right is almost hidden behind the riot of bright summer flowers. The man is Carl's father, old now and bent over his walking sticks. Carl's relationship with his father was strained, and when he included him in paintings, his father was often hidden or small in the background.

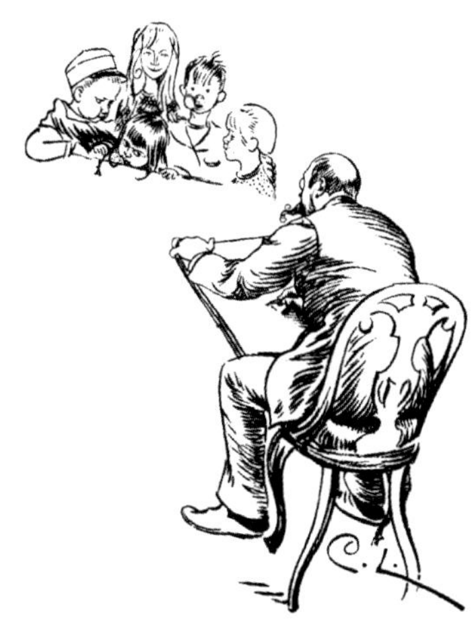

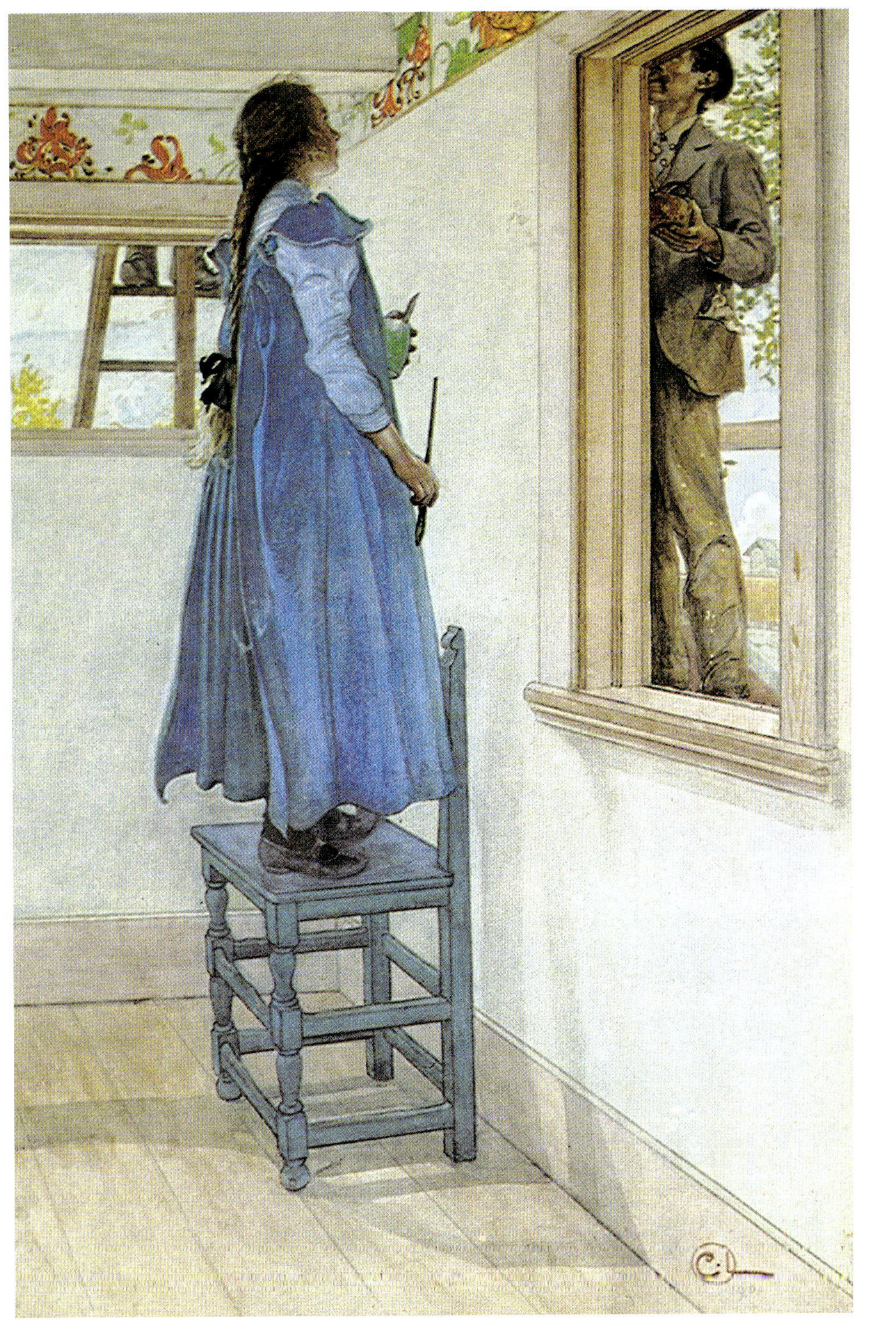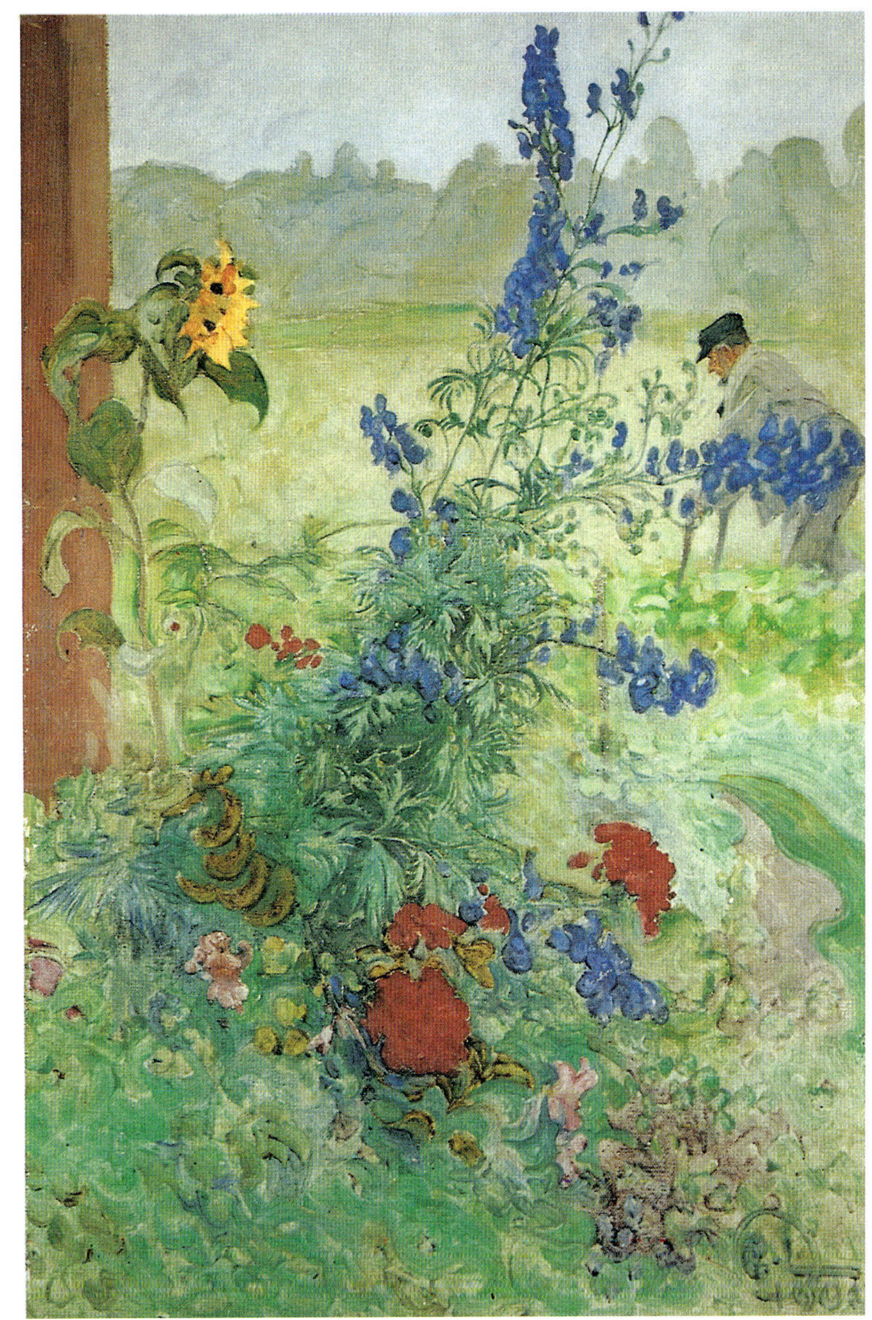

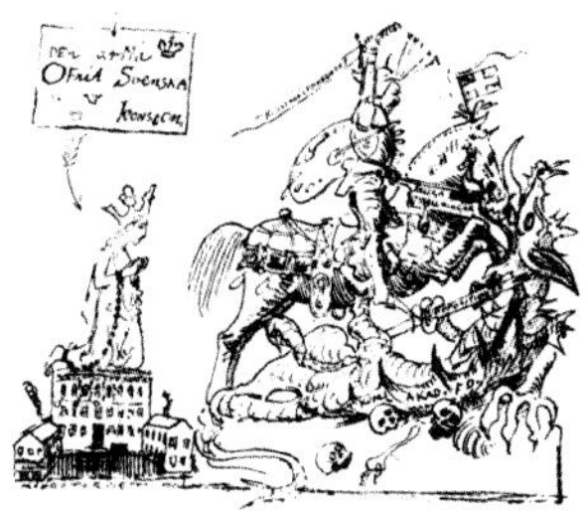

In 1903 Carl was commissioned to do a large painting for the assembly hall of a school in Gothenburg. He decided to base it on the story of St George and the Dragon, a theme he'd worked on before for an exhbition catalogue (from which the drawing on the left is taken). He began to sketch ideas, and Karin started work on costumes.

Then he changed his mind. One day in early summer he saw a line of children carrying flowers, going to decorate the local school for the last day before the holidays. This would be his picture, and there was no need for elaborate historical outfits. He used his own children and their friends as models: Lisbeth is carrying the wreath in the centre of the work; Brita is on her right with the big bunch of cornflowers, and Ulf is at the front dressed as a sailor boy, pulling a wheelbarrow of birch branches. The old man with the stick is Carl's father, once again with his face hidden.

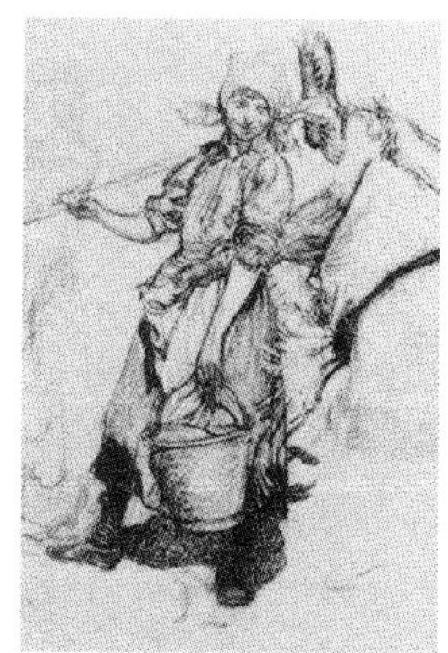

The painting is called *Outside Summer Winds Are Blowing;* it is 11 metres (36 feet) long and it still hangs in the same school in Gothenburg.

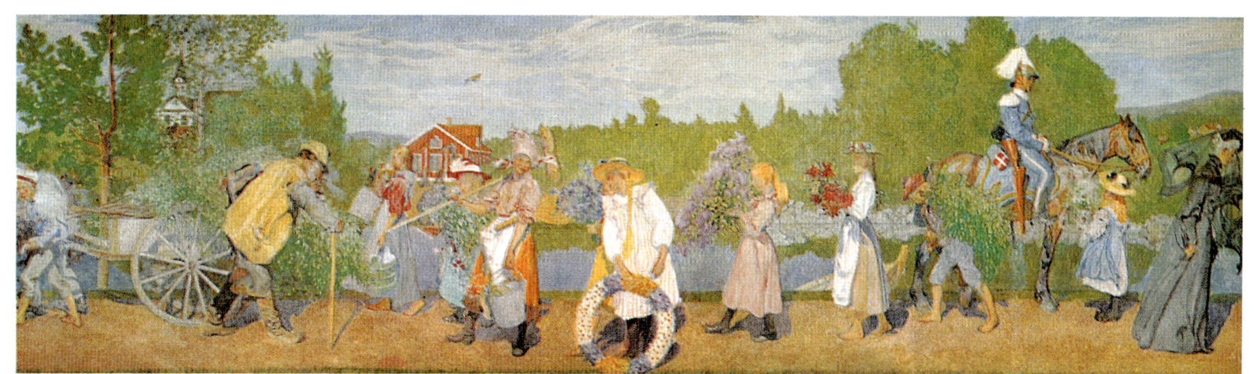

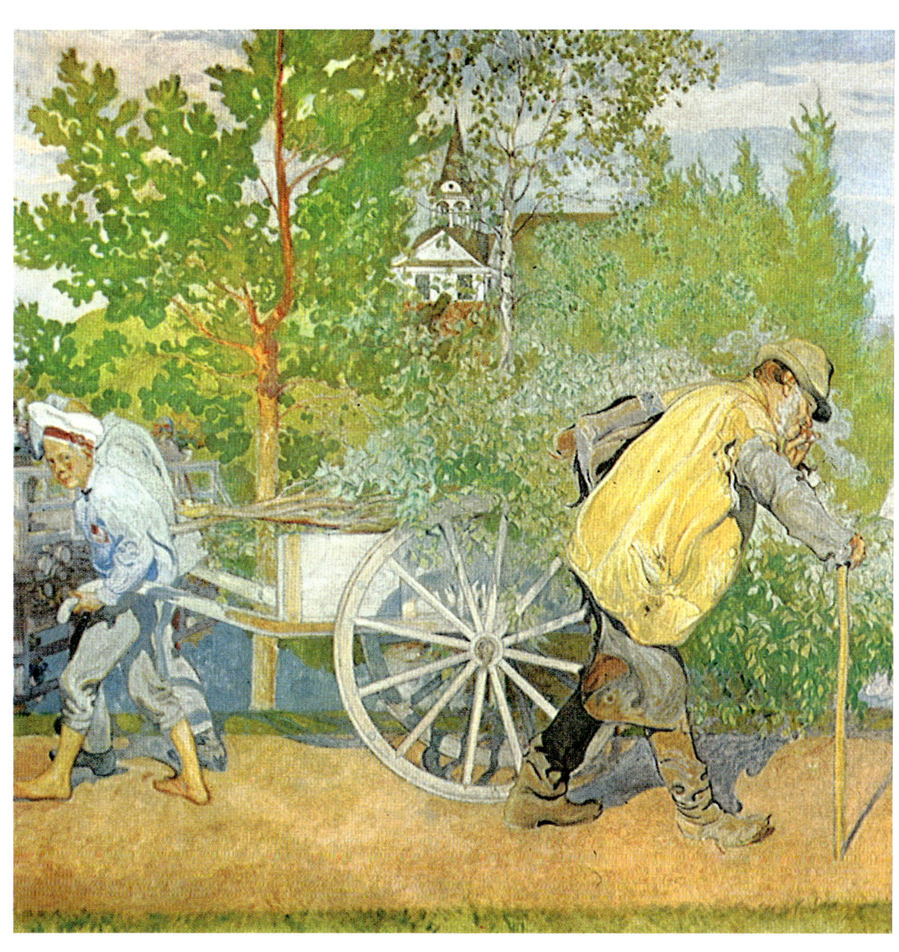

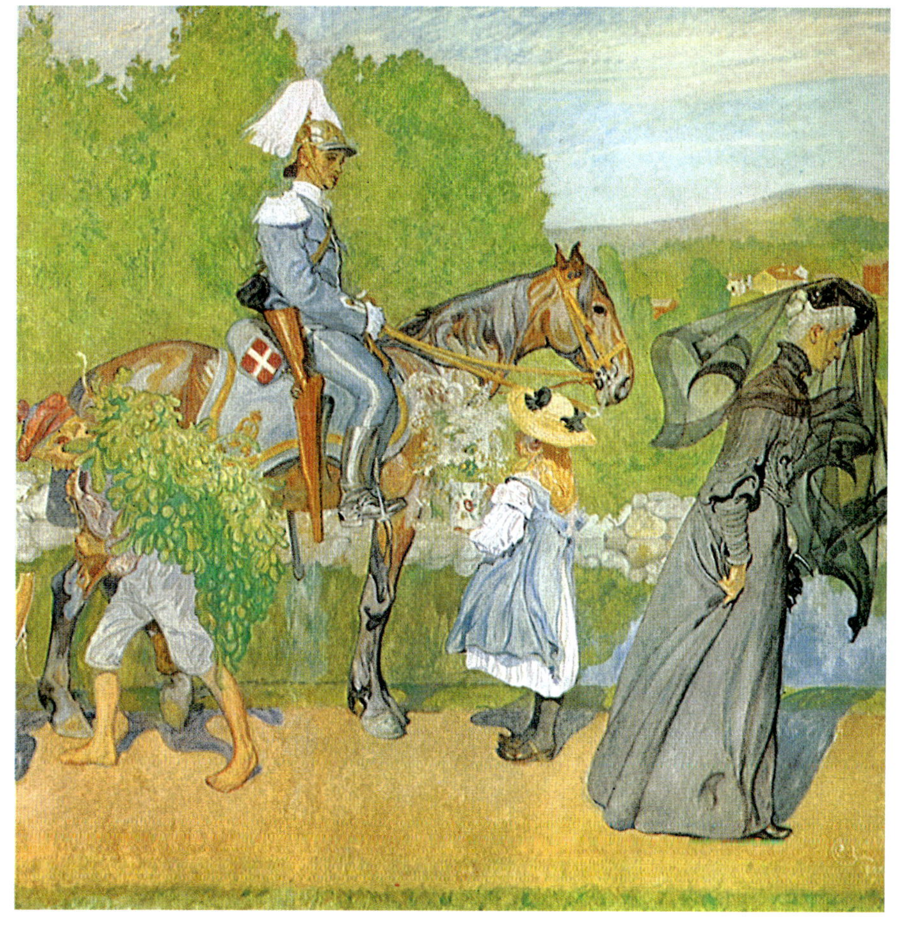

This watercolour, called *Mother and Daughter,* was also painted in 1903. It shows Karin, on the left, and Suzanne, now a young woman, standing in the middle of the floor. They appear to be in conversation, and Karin is deep in serious thought. By spacing the two figures apart, Carl brings a feeling of anxiety and awkwardness to the picture. Things were not always perfect in the Larsson household.

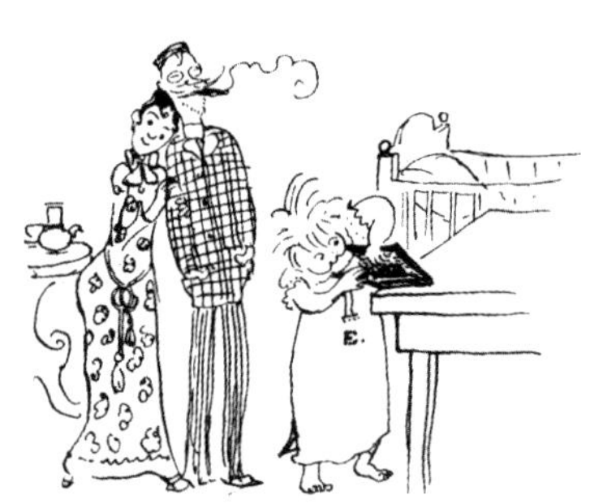

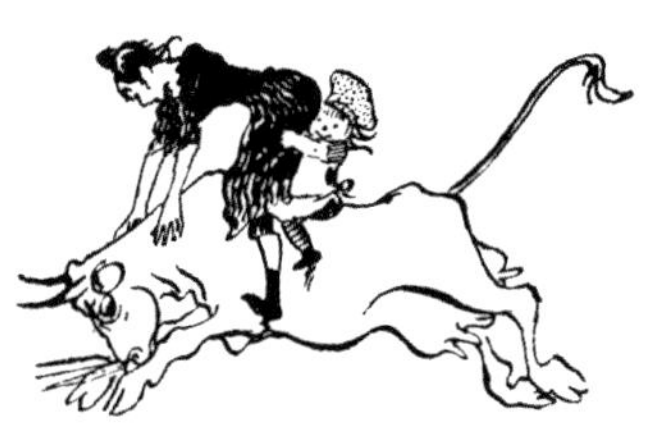

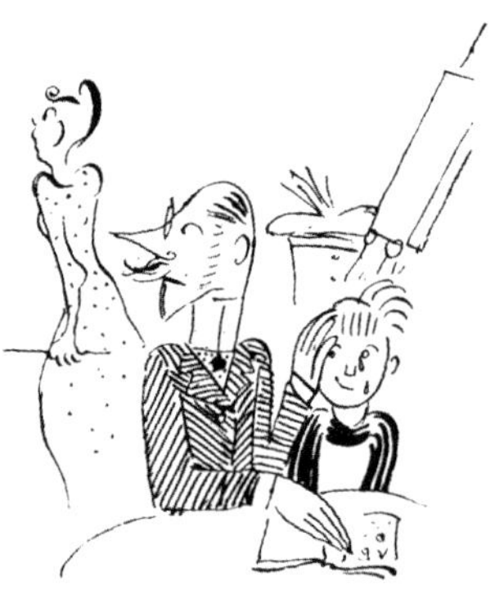

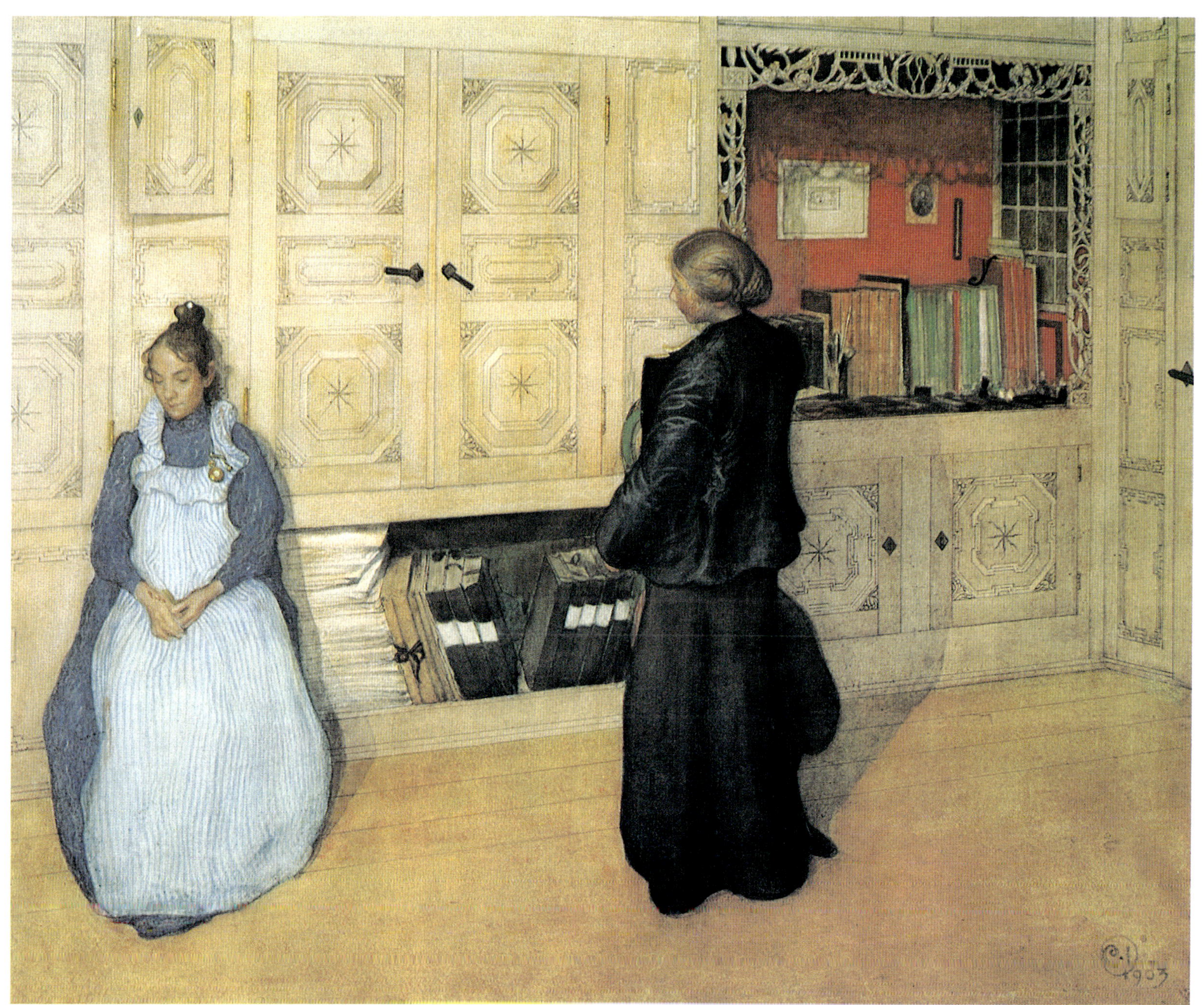

In 1905 Carl and Karin's oldest son Ulf died. He was not the first child they had lost: in 1894 a baby boy called Mats had died at the age of two months.

In *Karin on the Shore*, from 1908, Karin's black dress contrasts with the bright, late summer day. She is lost in thought, and hardly sees the brilliant red flowers, the sparkling water, or the girl with her dog in a rowing boat.

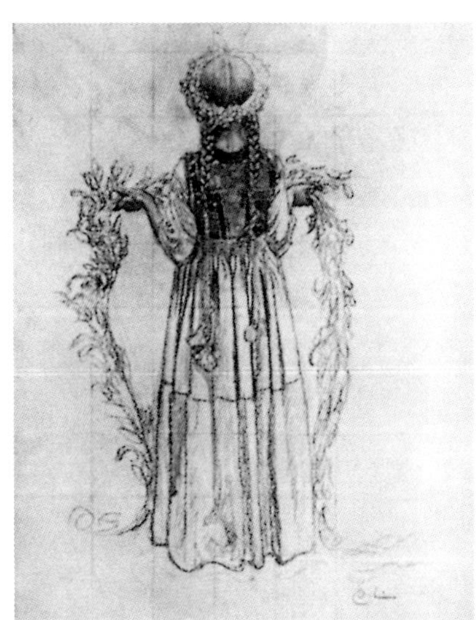

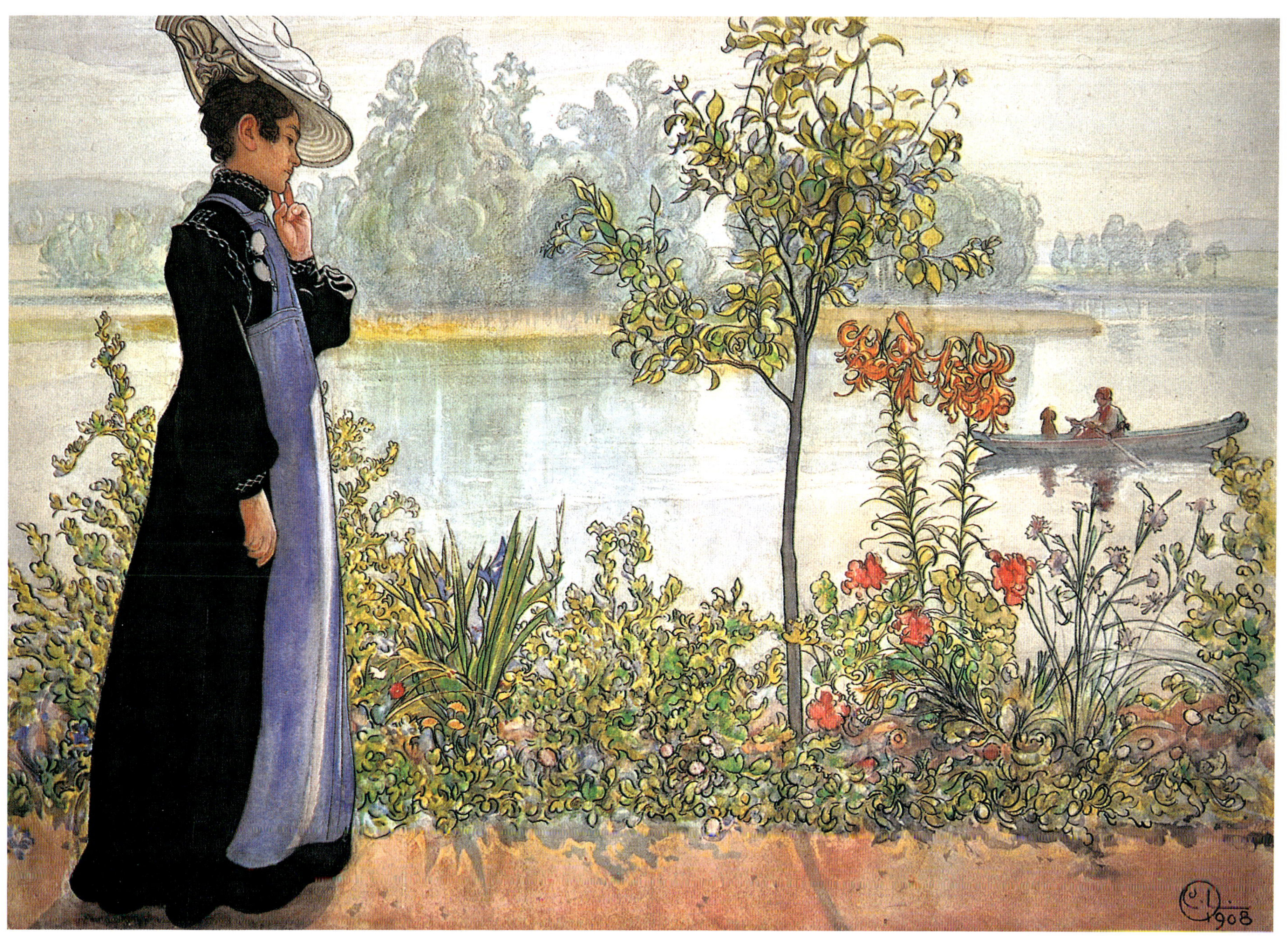

Ten years later and Esbjörn, the baby of the family, is now eighteen years old. This picture shows him sitting on the porch, reading, his feet leisurely resting against the paintwork. Although he was a good student, he loved to work on the farm at Spadarvet, and would do so after he finished school.

Throughout his life, Carl kept a family album of quick sketches. Some of the children's favourites were of Carl himself as a boy, and Carl would write humourous verses to go with them:

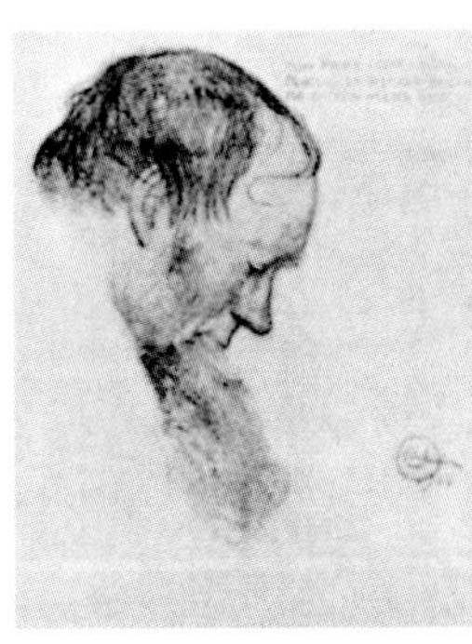

Out in the street, I kissed all the girls in sight,
I somehow seemed to think it was my right.
As for the boys, I simply boxed their ears,
And they ran home to mother, shedding tears.

I had to saw the firewood trim and neat,
But seldom got a crust of bread to eat.
I carried water for the women old,
And made a tidy heap of gold.

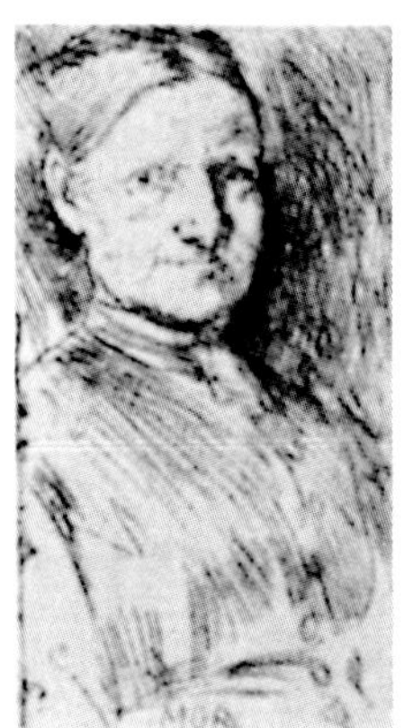

Our teacher shouted threats in my ear,
And pounded with a cane on my tender rear.
But when he saw my drawings, he cried out,
"Why, you're a genius, lad, and not a lout!"

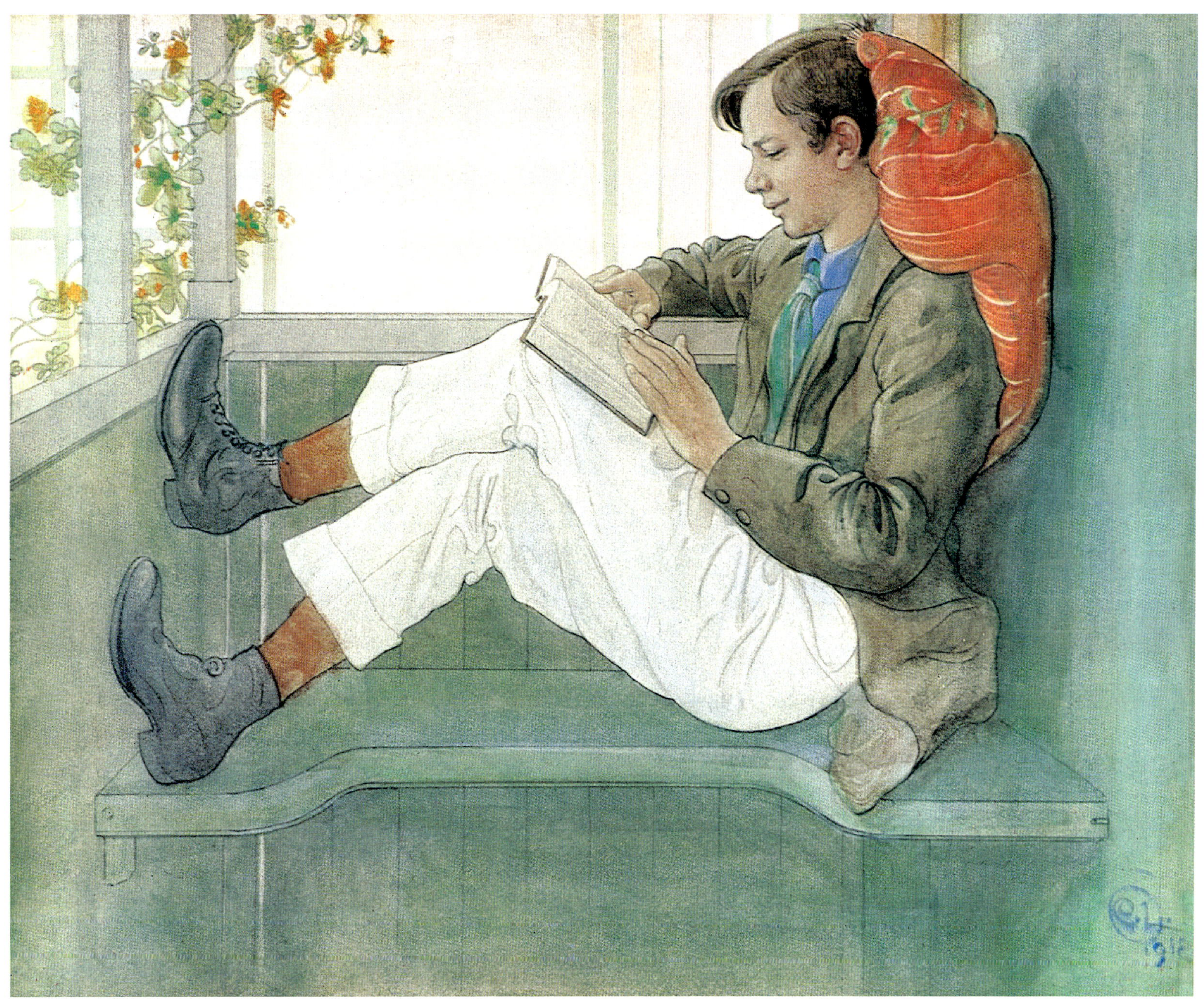

The portrait of Esbjörn on the porch, finished in 1918, turned out to be one of Carl's last paintings. He died on January 22, 1919 at the age of 66. His sketches and paintings of his family and home, though, survived the years, and offer a unique and remarkably intimate view of his life.

This painting, from Christmas Eve 1892, shows Suzanne, the two oldest boys and Lisbeth trying to hear what is going on behind the closed door. The sense of fun and mischief is unmistakeable. Beneath this picture, Carl wrote: "Memories of the little ones at Sundborn".

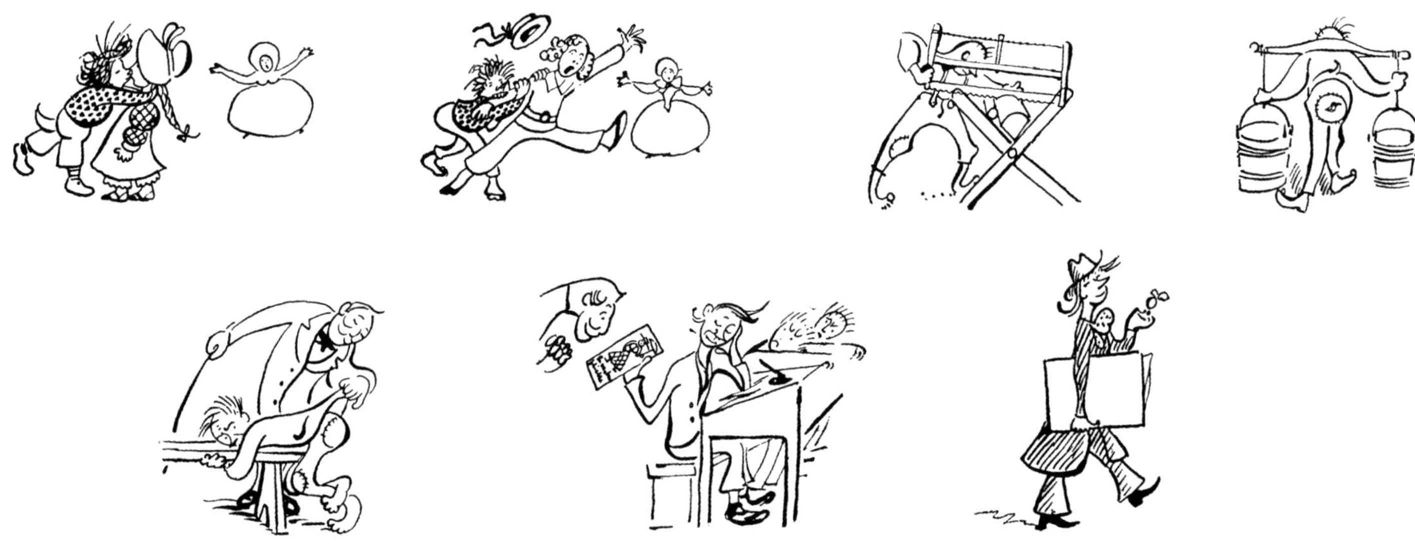

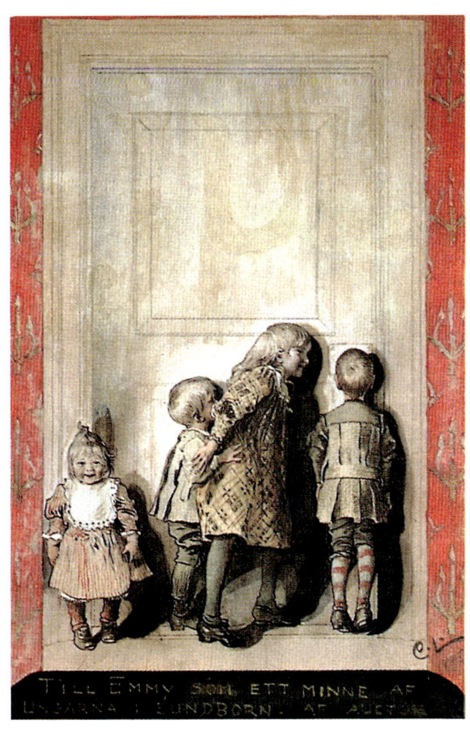

TILL EMMY SOM ETT MINNE AF
UNGARNA I LUNDBORN. AF AUCTOR

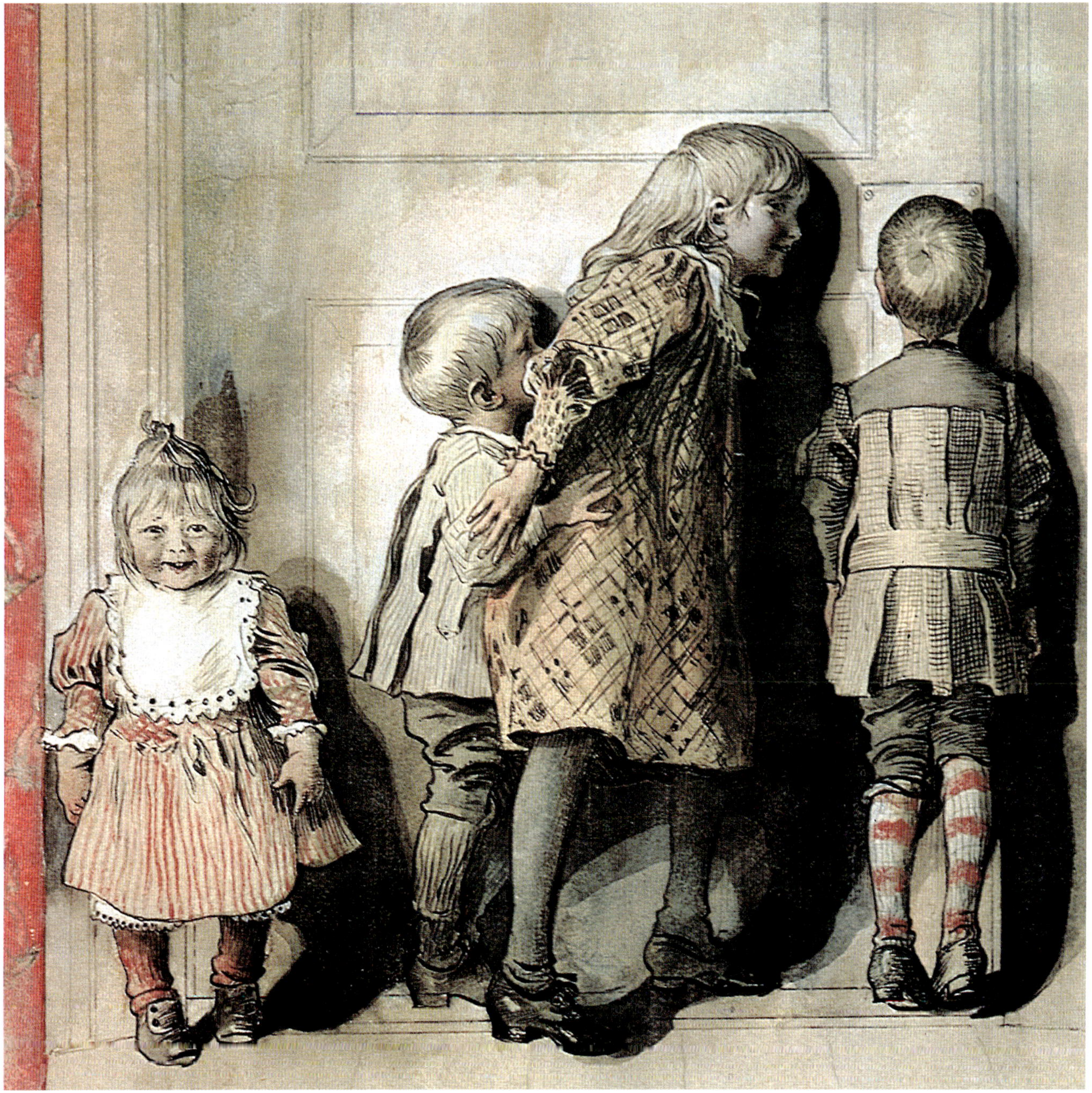

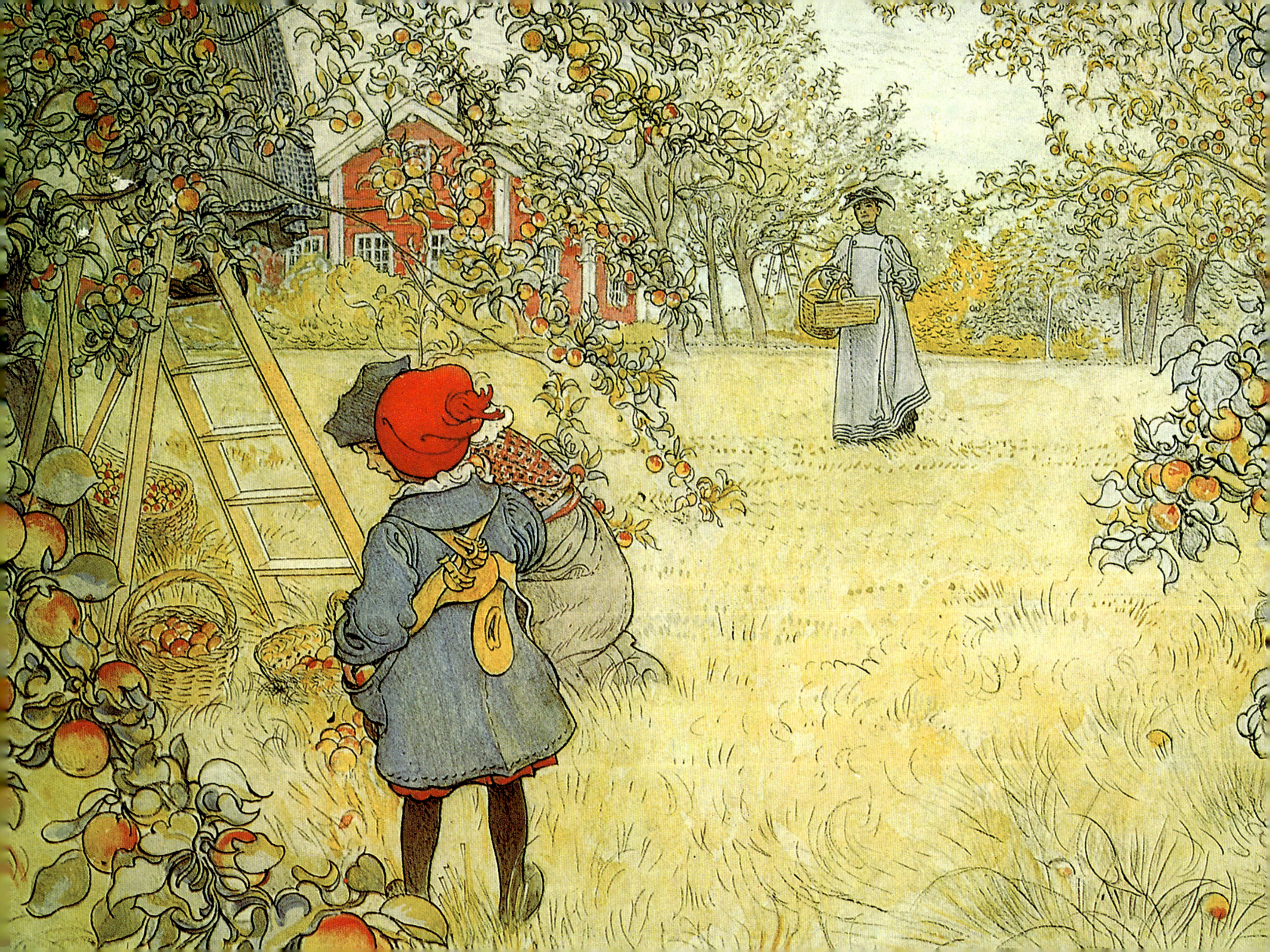

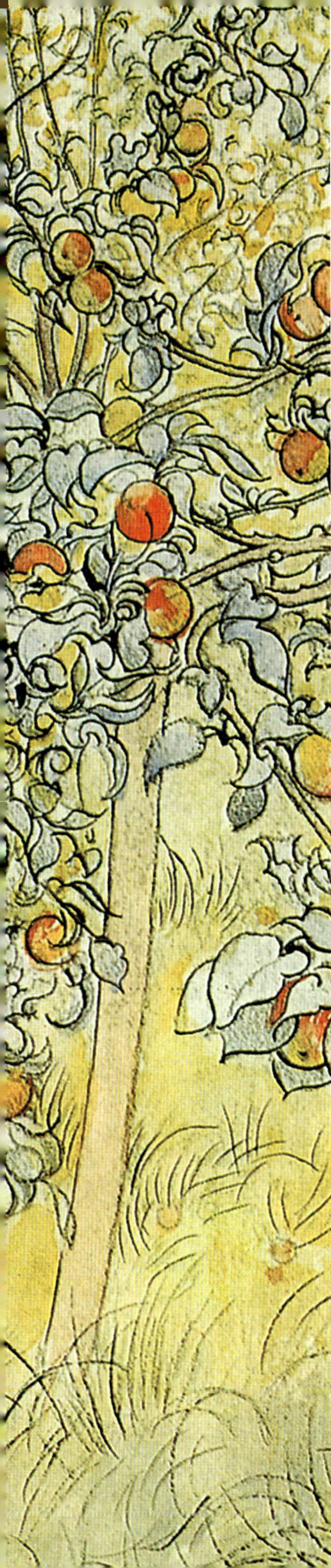

A FARM

Carl Larsson was born in Stockholm, but he wrote that if he had been born in the country, he would have become a farmer rather than an artist. As it was, he was an artist who longed to own a farm.

He and his family – his wife Karin, and their seven children – lived in a cottage called Lilla Hyttnäs (The Little Hut on a Point) in Sundborn, in the west of Sweden. One winter, Carl received a letter to say that the farm next door, called Spadarvet, was for sale. Included in the sale were four cows, one horse, one pig, some sheep, and chickens.

The Larsson family bought the farm in 1897, using money Carl had been paid for the large mural paintings at the National Museum in Stockholm. Carl wanted to continue to paint, so he hired Johan and his wife Johanna, who already lived at Spadarvet, to manage the farm. Tekla and Bäckström from the village joined the staff as well.

This first painting shows the artist at work, sketching on the hill. Johanna and Blossom the cow came by at just the right time to be included in the picture.

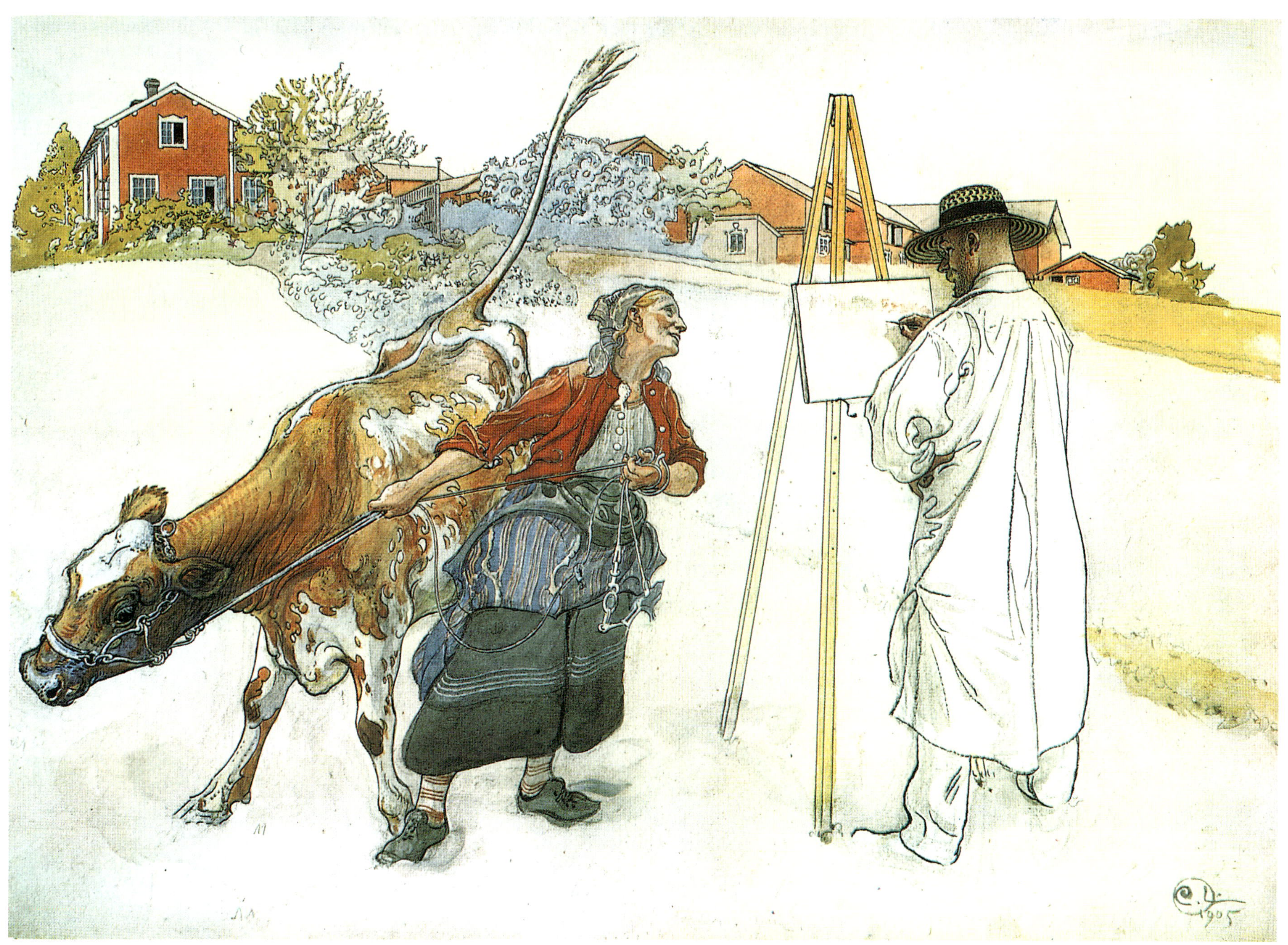

This picture shows how hard farm work was in the depths of winter. The trees around the farm weren't large, so the wood could only be used for firewood. Nonetheless, the cows needed grazing land so Johan and Bäckström went out with their tools to clear some space.

First they built a fire for warmth, and put on the coffee pot, which can be seen in the background. The trees were felled and trimmed, and lifted onto the sawbuck where Johan can be seen sawing them into uniform lengths. Bäckström then split the thickest logs with an axe and wedge and stacked them neatly, bark-side up to protect against the rain. Winter days are short in Sweden, so they worked quickly.

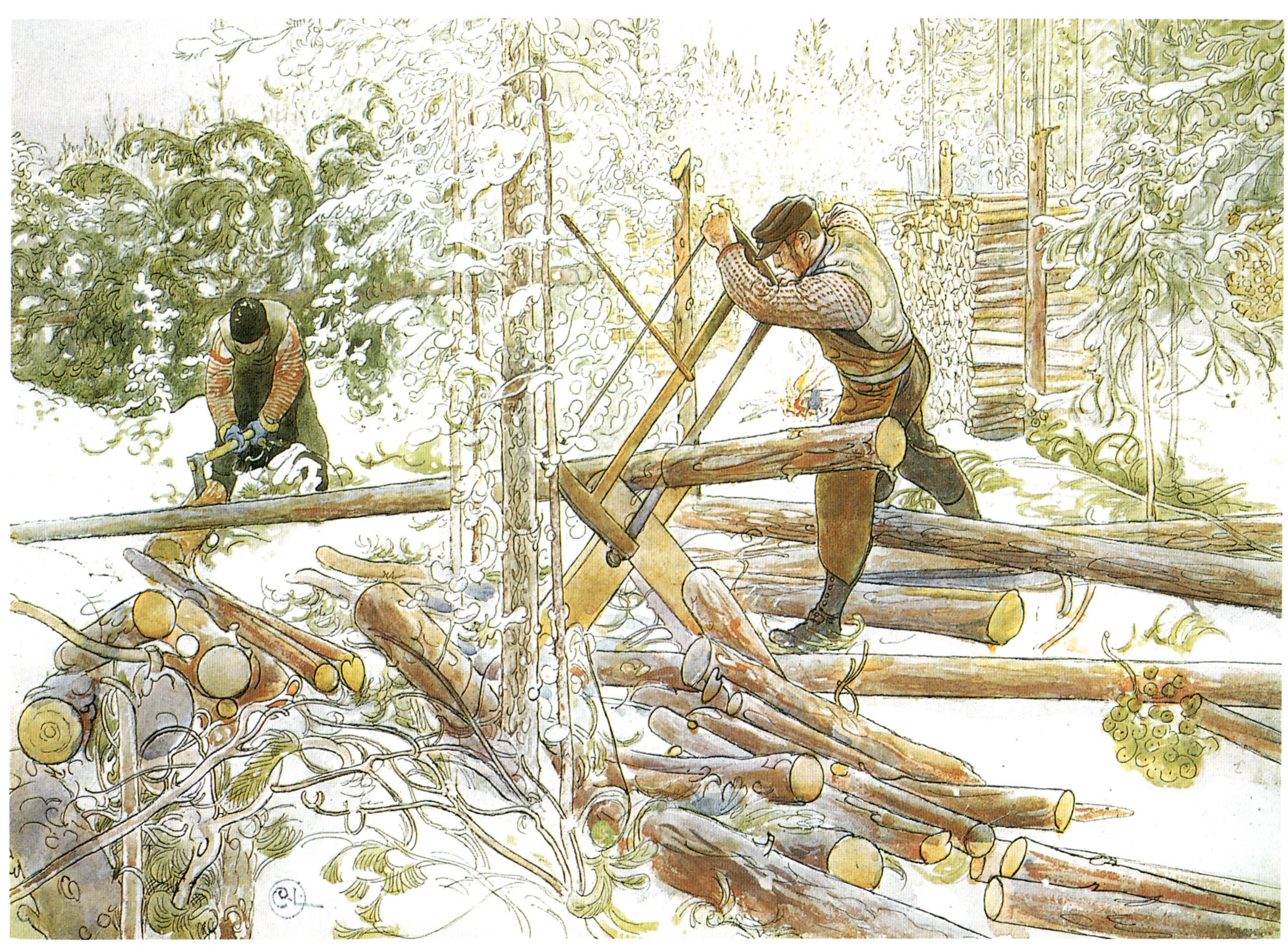

There were no refrigerators in Carl Larsson's day, so ice was collected from the lakes in the winter, to use for preserving food in the summer. The ice had to be cut and stored before the end of February to ensure it was hard and crystal clear; that way it would last for several months.

This painting again shows Johan and Bäckström hard at work outdoors. (Carl would have done a sketch outdoors, and then finished the painting in the warmth of his studio.) They hitched Brunte the horse to the sleigh and drove to Lake Toftan. They took ice saws with them, which were more than six feet long, and had teeth two and a half inches in size. They also took boat hooks, and the ever-present coffee pot.

They made a hole and eased the point of the saw down into the ice, then sawed off hugh blocks of ice which bobbed about in the water. Then they fastened the hooks under the first block, and one by one Brunte heaved them out of the water. Before they left, they put pine branches around the openings in the ice, so no one would fall in.

Back at the farm, the ice was covered in a layer of fine, dry sawdust, about twenty inches thick, to keep it frozen.

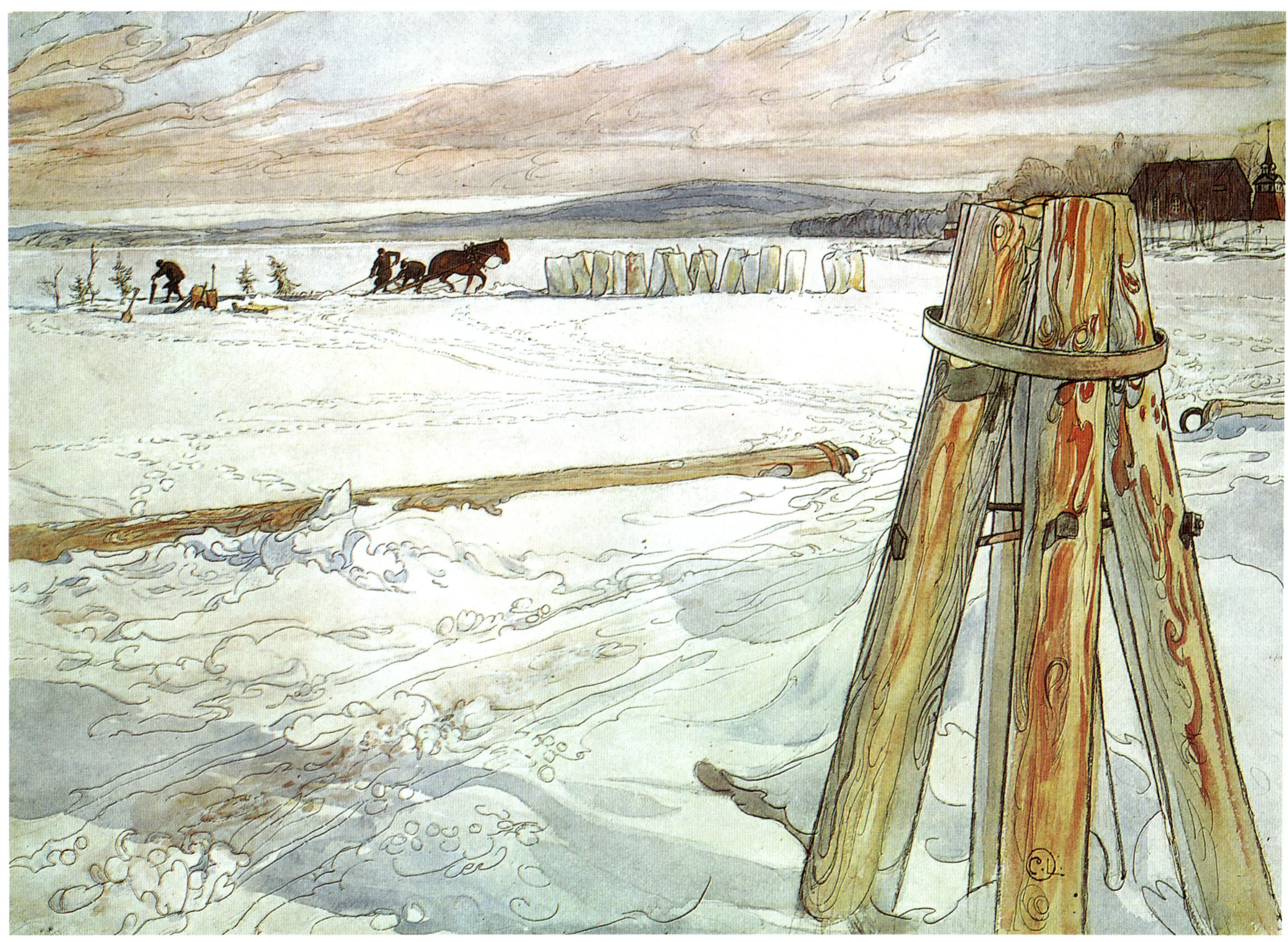

When the weather was bad over the winter, Johan would often work in the carpenter's shed. Before spring came, everything on the farm – roofs, fences, sleighs, ploughs – had to be inspected to see what needed to be repaired. Every farm had a carpenter's shed where new furniture and tools were made. Many farms also had a forge where they mended wagon wheels and forged axes, spades, chisels and hammers. Everything was made to last.

In this painting, Esbjörn, Carl and Karin's youngest son, is helping with the woodwork. The workshop is filled with tools – axes, saws, planes, chisels and drills – but Esbjörn likes the fine, sharp knife for carving most of all. Here, he is asking Johan to help him mend his wooden spade, because the handle has come off.

The pair are surrounded by wood shavings. There were a lot of birch trees in the local area, so birch was often used in woodwork, but even Esbjörn would have been able to tell from the smell of the shavings whether they might instead be juniper or pine.

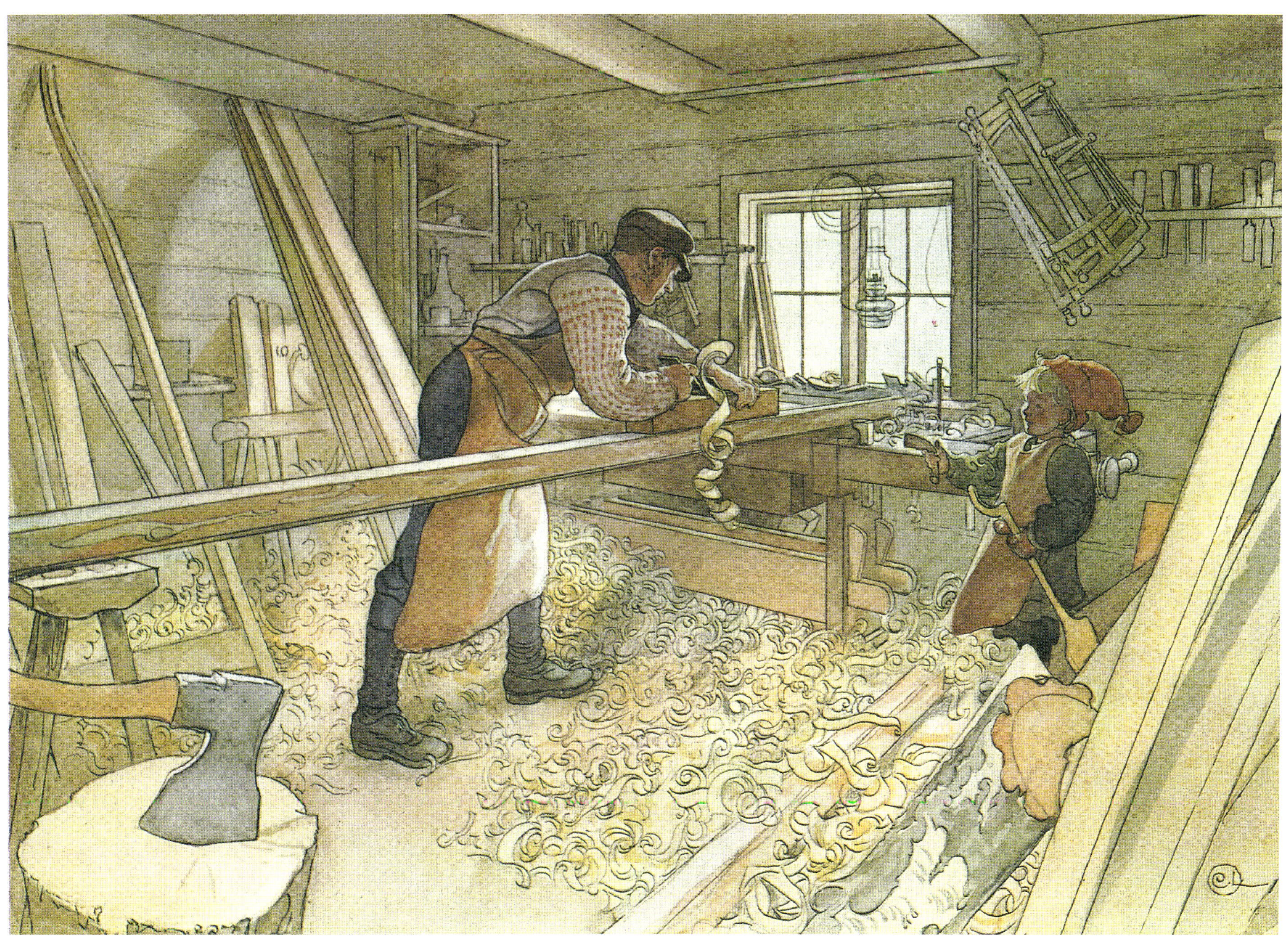

A Swedish farmer also had to be a fisherman, as well as a carpenter and blacksmith. Every morning during April, come shine or icy rain, Johan fished off Bullerholmen, the island visible across the lake from the Larsson's house. He often caught perch and a kind of fat carp, as well as small pike. Fishing in bad weather was not easy, and a sudden gust of wind could send the small boat careering across the bay.

Johan can be seen here pulling a pike from the net – some perch are already in the boat – and inspecting the net for damage. Nets were regularly repaired, but when they got too worn, new ones were made. On the right of the picture is a bow net, a kind of long sack that the fish swam into and then couldn't escape from. Bow nets were usually left lying in places where the fish were known to swim in spring.

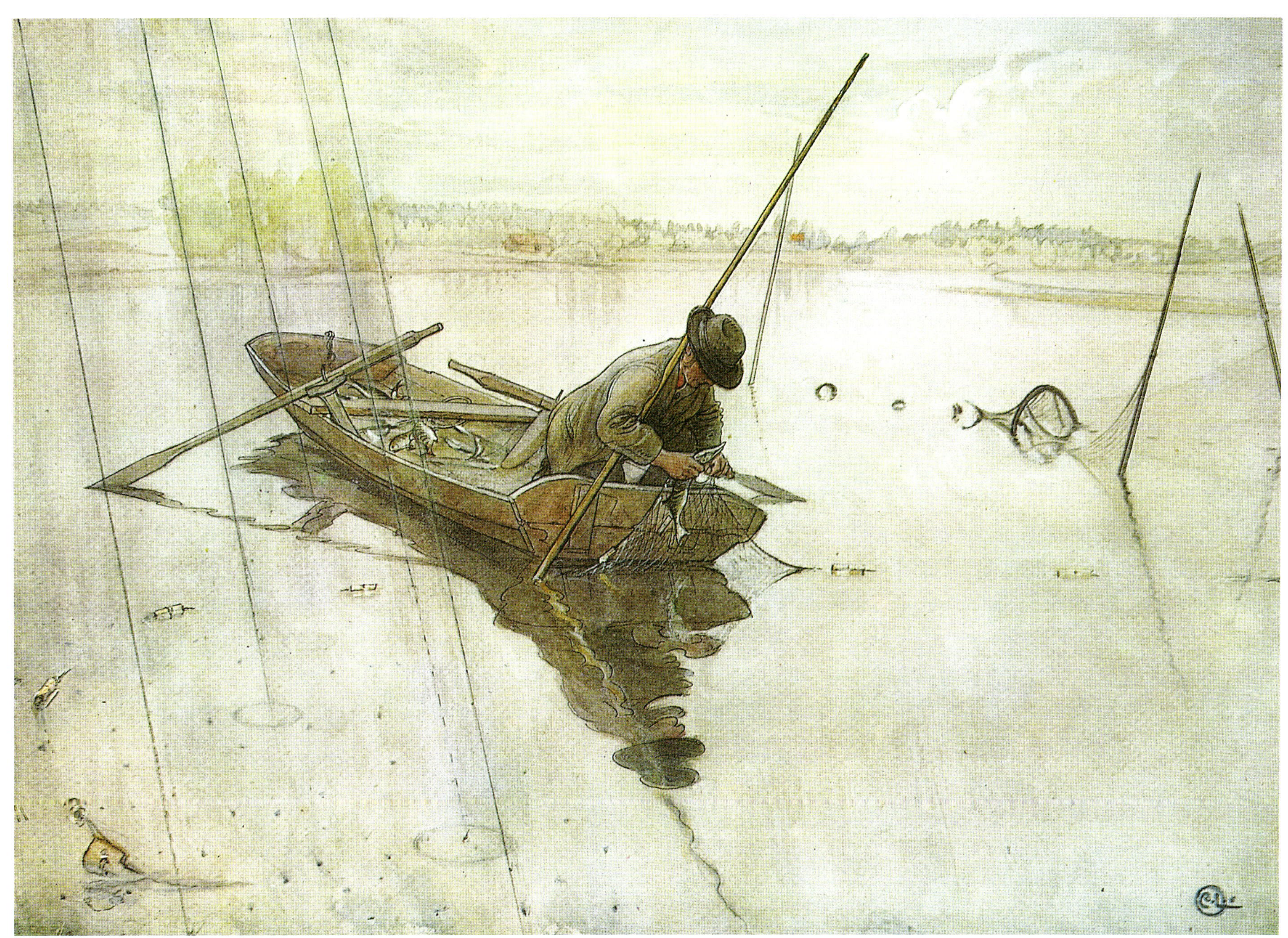

Finally, spring arrived at Spadarvet. New leaves are just visible on the birch tree in this picture. In May, as the weather turned, Johan would decide when it was time to start harrowing the fields. This field has been pasture land, with grass growing for several years. In the previous autumn it was ploughed under and lay fallow over the winter. Now it's time to sow the oats.

First, the ground had to be harrowed thoroughly to break up the soil. Johan and Bäckström hitched Brunte to the new, heavier spring-tooth harrow, while Lisa, the smaller horse, pulled the lighter one. The harrows were drawn over the ground three or four times. Tekla, the farm girl, followed on behind, breaking up any remaining lumps by hand. It was hot, tiring work. When they had finished, the crows and gulls would swoop onto the field, feasting on the worms and grubs turned up by the harrow.

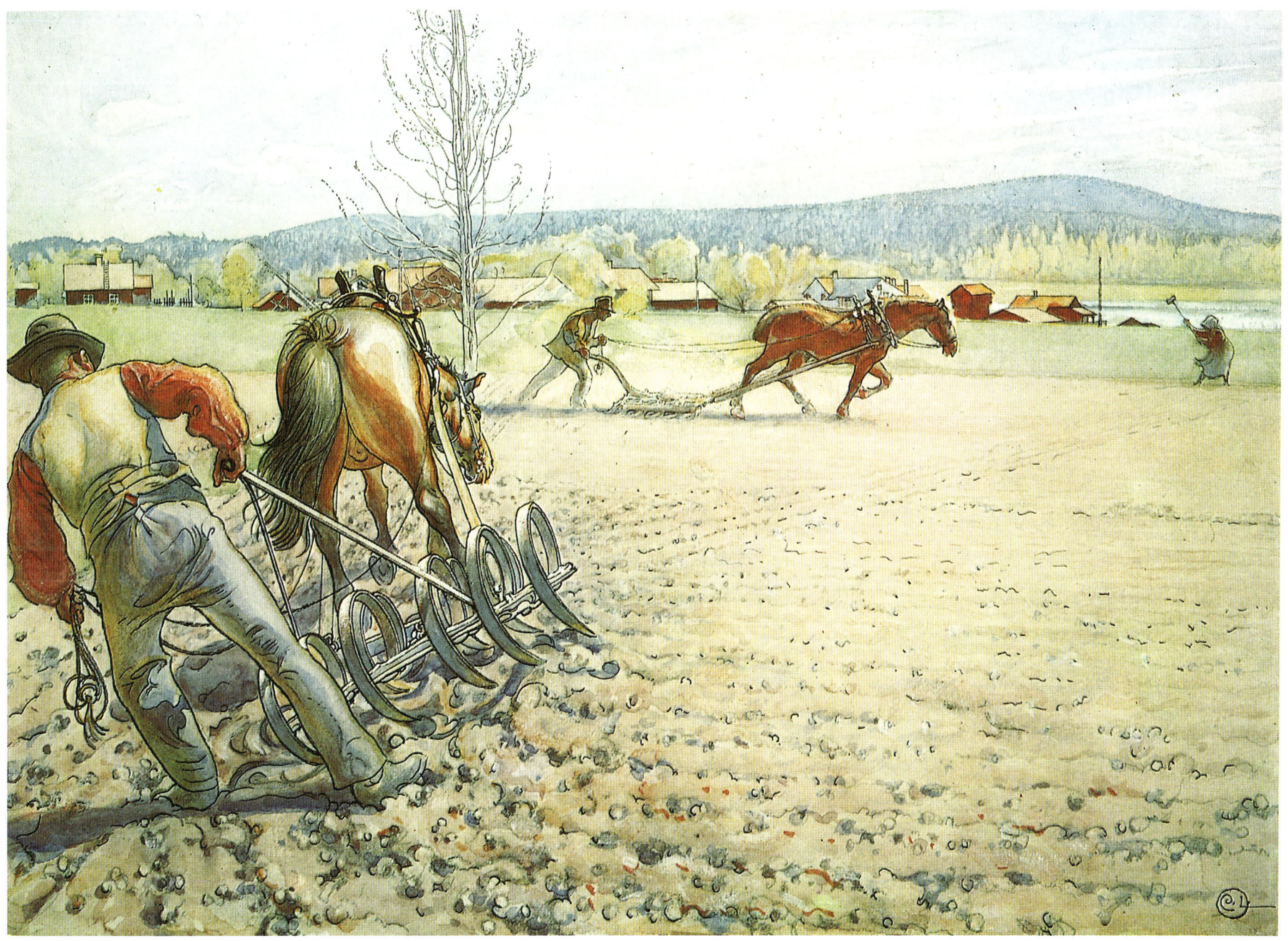

This painting is set later that same day. Johan, Tekla and Bäckström have had their evening meal, fed the horses, and have now returned to work to start the job of sowing the oats. Bäckström hitched Brunte to the light harrow and continued harrowing; they can be seen in the background of the picture. In the foreground are Johan and Tekla. They loaded the bags of oats into an open-sided wagon, which Lisa the mare pulled to the birch grove.

In those days, there were no machines for sowing seed; it had to be done by hand, and was a very skilled job – usually carried out by the farmer himself. The seed had to fall evenly on the ground, to ensure an even crop. Johan carried the oats in a big open bag fastened to him by straps, so that both hands were free to scatter the seed. First the right hand, then the left, would move in large arcs, the seed falling in a rhythmic pattern. Tekla kept him supplied with new seed.

The sinking sun behind him casts a long, blue shadow. As it got dark, Johan stopped sowing and lightly harrowed the seed, to keep it moist and to stop the birds from eating it. Bäckström and Brunte ploughed late into the night.

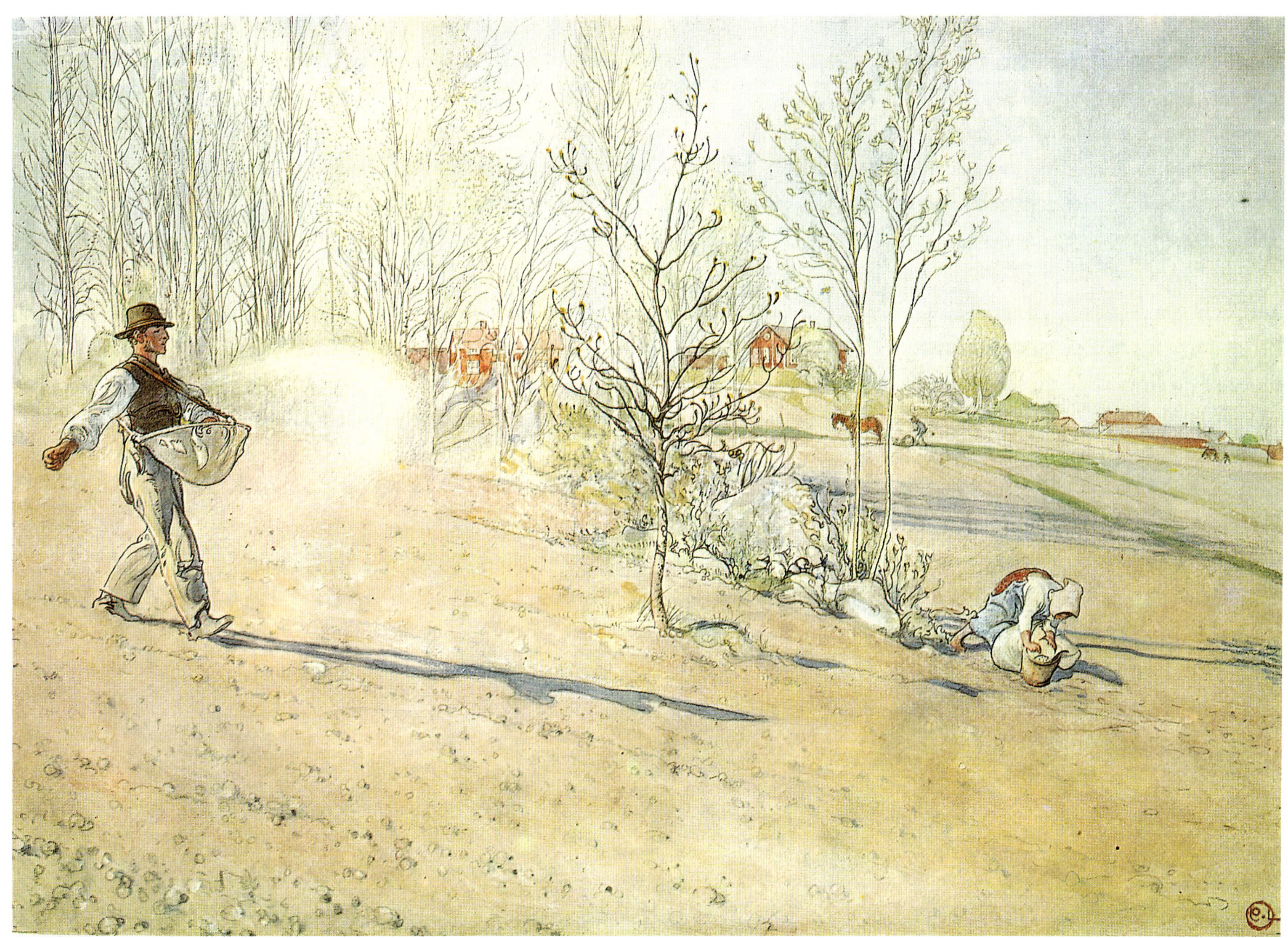

The first real summer rain arrived, and it left the meadows and woods smelling fragrant and sweet. The birches were in full leaf and the swallows had returned. Johanna decided it was time to put the cows out to pasture.

In Sweden, cows have to be shut up for the long winter months, so when they are finally let out, they go wild. Their tails go straight up in the air and they bound about, mooing and charging each other playfully.

In this picture, Tekla and the youngest Larsson daughter, Kersti, have taken the cows to graze in the woods. To entice the cows along, Tekla would sing and call; shepherd girls and boys often kept salt in their pockets as well, which the cows liked. Blossom, the bell cow, came first, then the others followed. Kersti waved a willow stick from behind to keep them moving.

On the day Carl Larsson sketched this painting, Tekla has brought a ribbon loom with her to help pass the time. Her bare feet are warmed by the summer sun. Kersti is sitting on a rock in the background, as Krusa the cow noses in her pocket for salt.

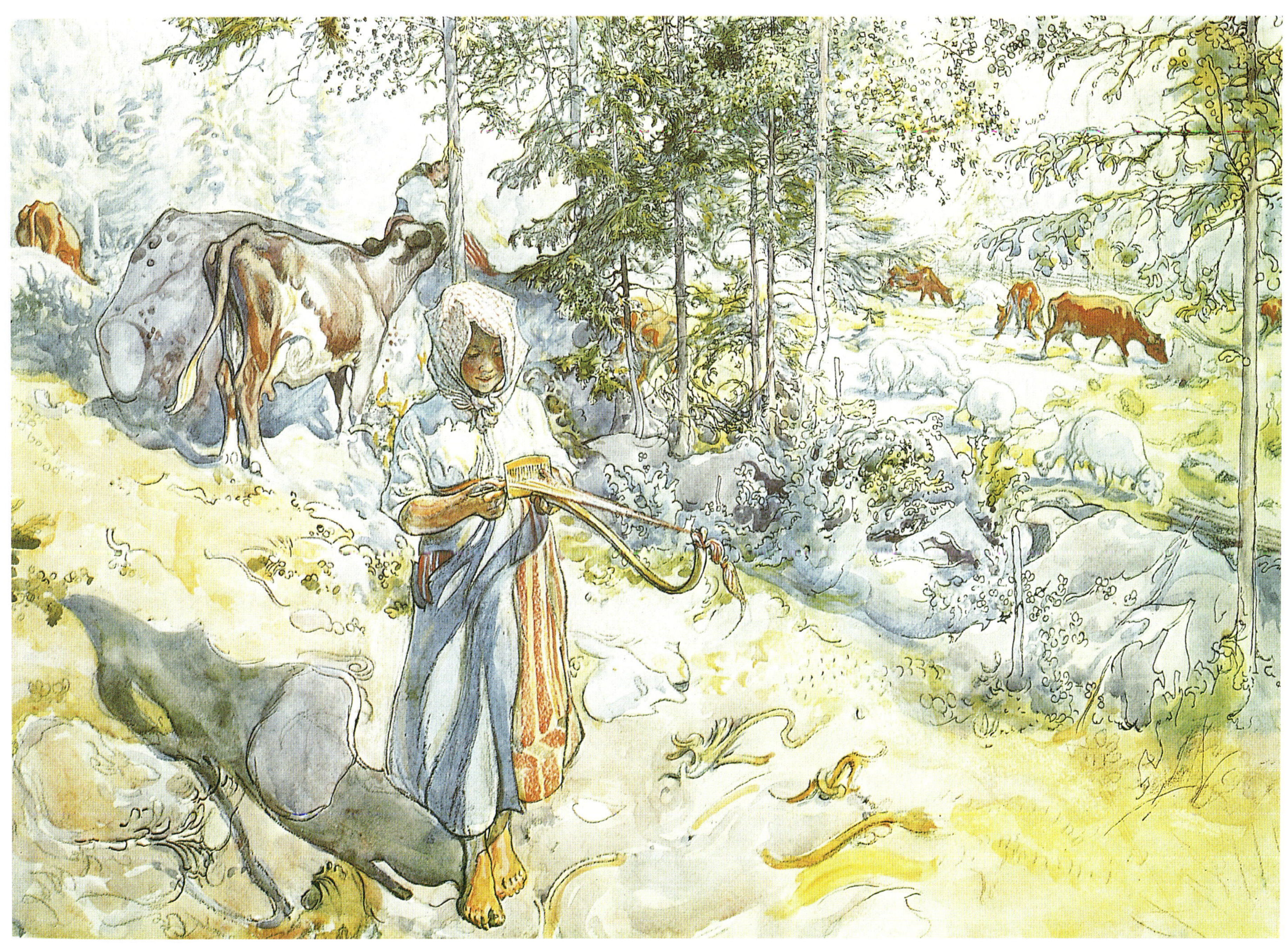

Sometimes, the cows would be milked out on the hill then left to return to the woods overnight. On this day, though, they were taken home and milked in their stalls. Johanna milked into a large well-scrubbed bucket, sitting on her milking stool, and here she is milking Krusa. First she would wipe the udder, then grease the teats, and then start milking.

On the left of the painting is a large red water pump to fill the cows' troughs with water. For the time, this was a very modern device and saved having to bring water from a well. There's also a birch broom for sweeping out the stalls, which Johanna did every evening after milking was finished. She also spread fresh straw onto the floor, and gave the sheep hay and grain.

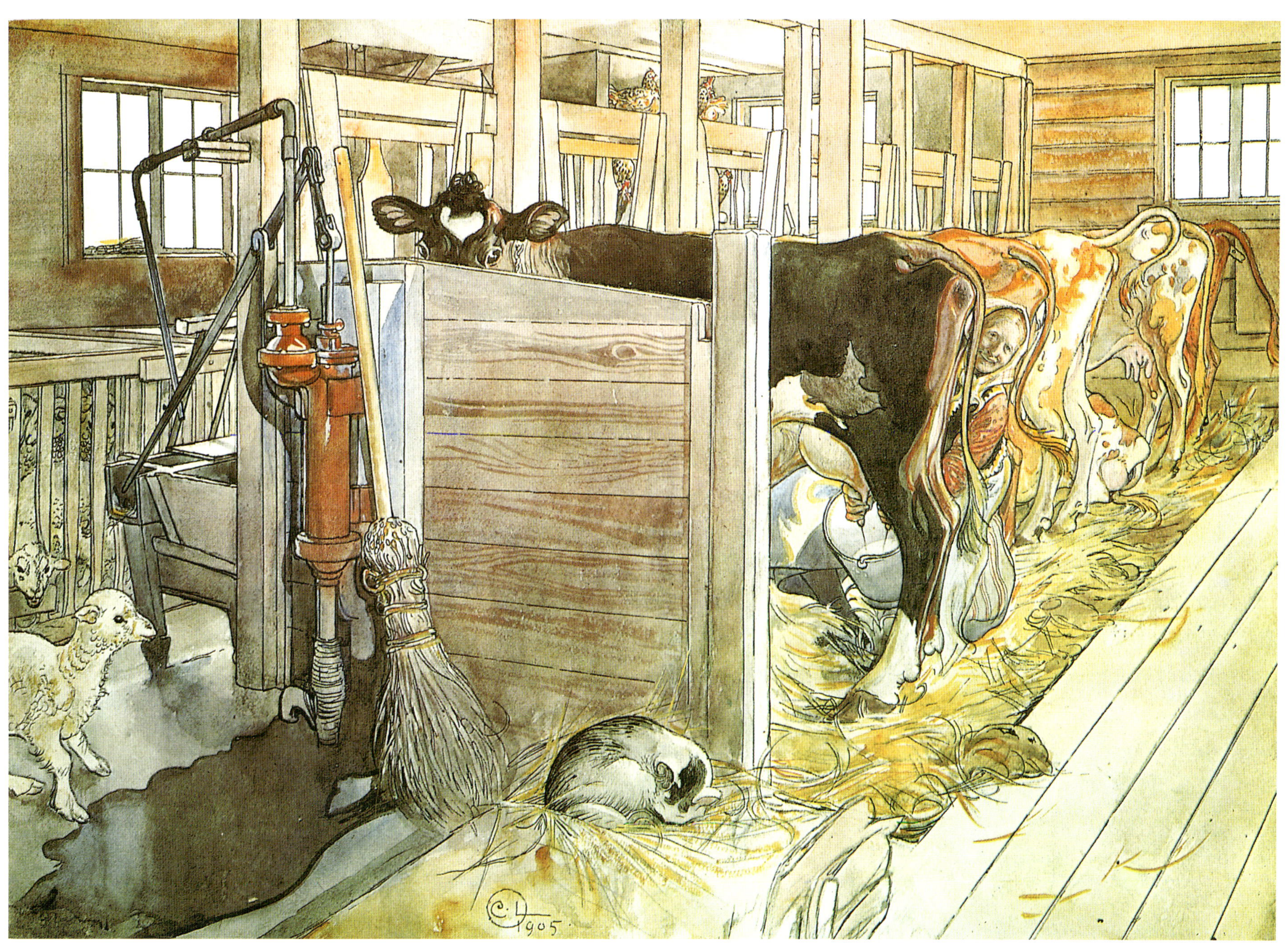

It was now the first week in July, and in Sundborn it was time to start harvesting.

When Carl Larsson painted these four pictures, they had just bought a new mowing machine, much faster than using a scythe. Brunte pulled the device and Johan bobbed up and down on the little seat. It cut through everything: grass, ox-eye daisies, buttercups and harebells. On the left-hand side of the first painting, Bäckström and Lisa are operating the drag rake while Johanna and Tekla rake up anything that's left by hand.

Only the rye still had to be cut with a scythe, as shown in the second painting, because it needed to be bound into sheaves. The third picture shows the dusty work of threshing, done later in the autumn. Brunte was hitched up just outside the barn door, and acted as a motor for the threshing machine, walking round in a circle. Tekla collected the sheaves and threw them to Johan, who fed them into the machine. Johanna raked away the straw and Bäckström gathered it together on a hay fork and threw it up to the boys in the hayloft.

Finally came the winnowing, separating the grain from the chaff. The Larssons had a lovely blue winnowing machine, a relatively new invention which replaced thrashing the grain by hand. The heavy grain seeds fell near the machine, while the lighter chaff floated away. The hens had to be regularly chased away from the seed.

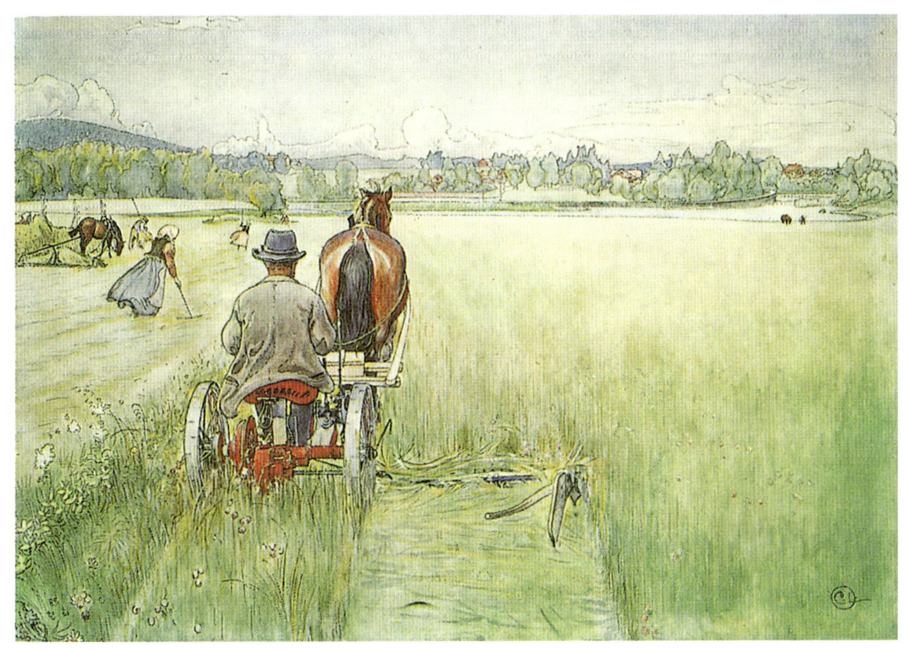
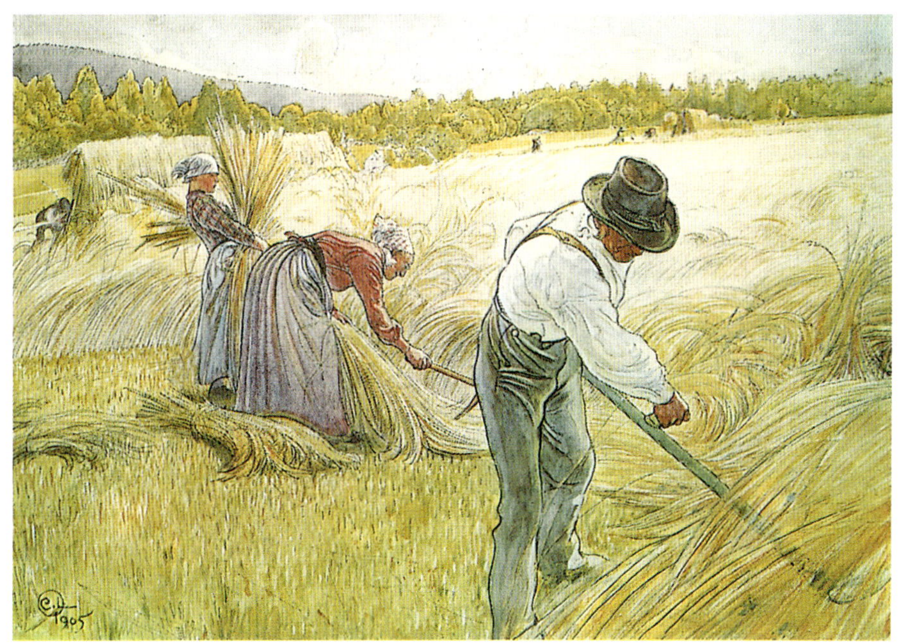
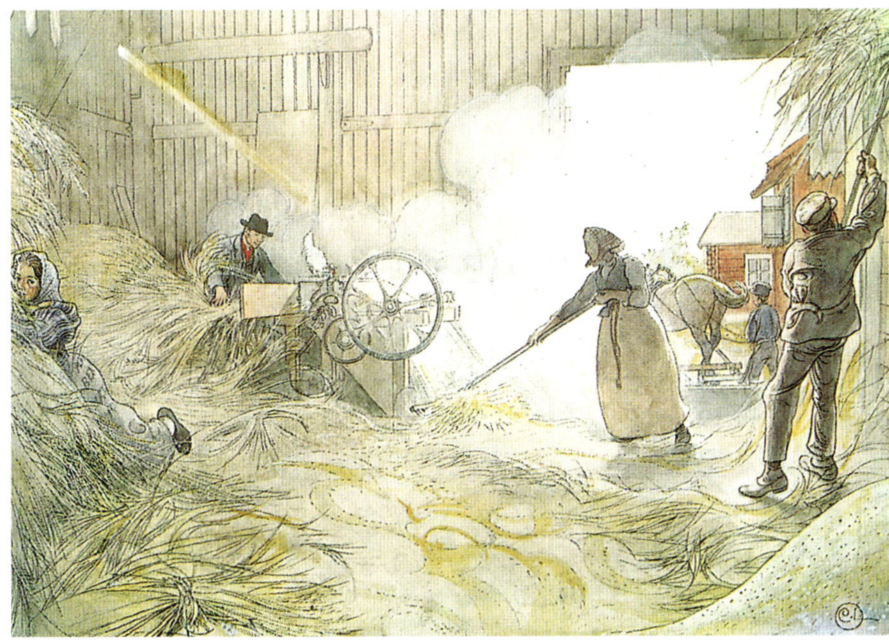
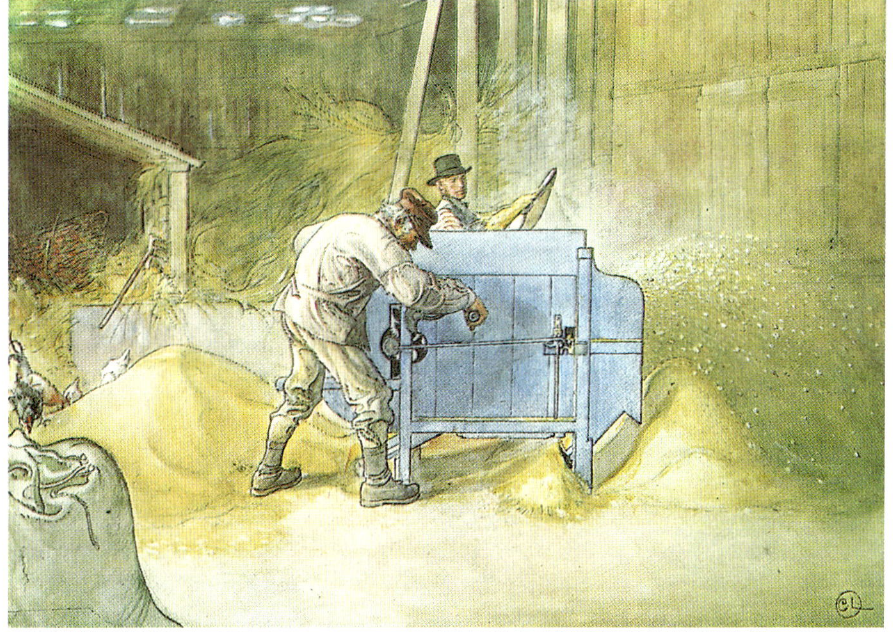

Even on Sundays, farmers sometimes had to work. On the day of this painting of the church in Sundborn, Johan and Bäckström had arrived late because one of the cows had calved that morning. They're sitting at the back rather than in their usual pew. In traditional churches like this one, women, girls and small children sat on the left-hand side of the aisle, while the men and boys sat on the right. Although he was only young – his head barely reaches the top of the pew – Esbjörn was proud to sit with the men, just in front of Johan.

The man at the back in the blue cape is the churchwarden, holding an offertory bag. In earlier days, his job was as a 'rouser' to waken anyone who fell asleep during the sermon.

The paintings of the angels and dove above the altar at the front were done by Carl Larsson.

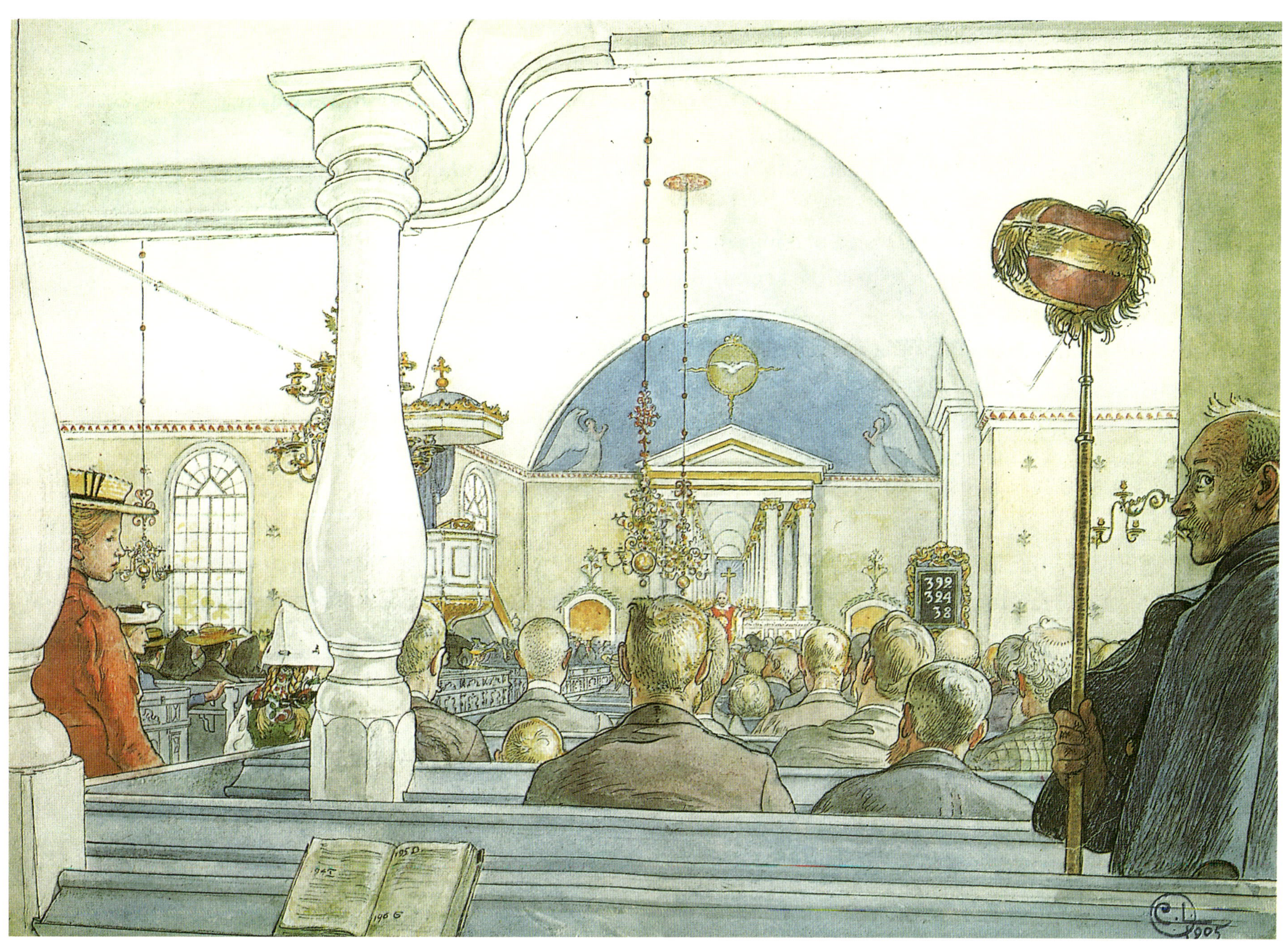

Over the winter, a large amount of manure accumulated in the barn, the stalls and the pigpens. It was all deposited in the dung yard, and left on the ground to draw out the acids. Too much sunlight, though, could dry out the precious fertiliser, and too much rain could make it too weak. In this painting, therefore, Elfström, one of the farm-hands, is building a more permanent enclosure to shelter the manure.

The compost heap was covered with earth or straw to keep the smell in. The hens and the rooster love the compost heap almost as much as they love the winnowed grain. Here, the rooster stands proud on one leg, complaining about the invasion of his space.

Bäckström is forking the well-rotted manure into a cart in the background. Further away, a flag on a neighbouring building signals a special event: it was Johanna's birthday, and everyone was going to celebrate that afternoon.

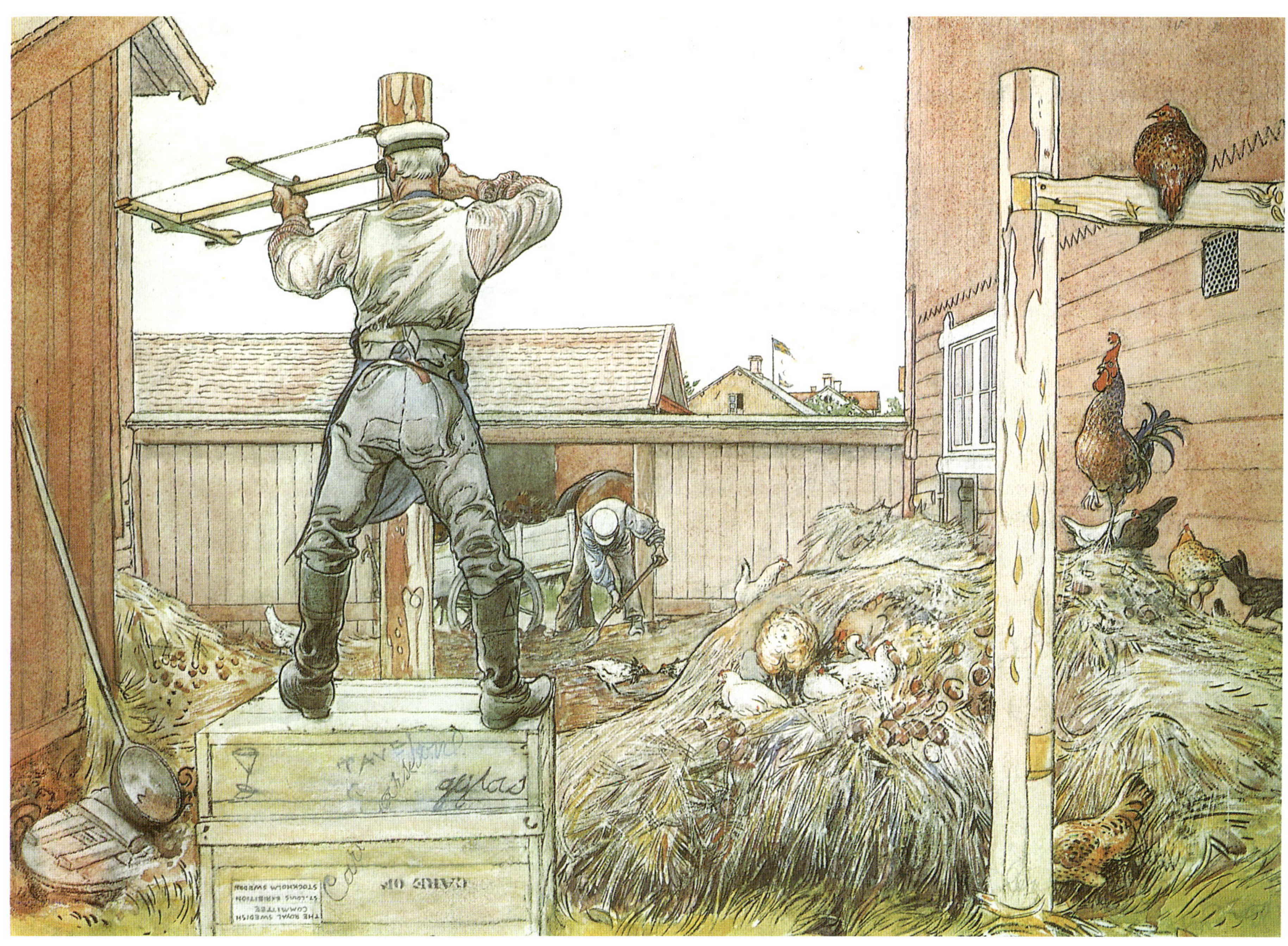
glas
GARD OF
THE ROYAL SWEDISH
COMMITTEE
ST. LOUIS EXHIBITION
STOCKHOLM SWEDEN

During the previous winter, Johan and Bäckström had already carted some manure out to a field that had been lying fallow for a year. They had made several large piles, and covered them with earth to protect them. Now it was time to spread the manure around the field and harrow it in, before sowing the rye.

It was heavy, dirty work, but Johan was very strong and could keep going until all the manure was spread. In autumn, tender rye shoots would appear and they would be safe under the snow all winter.

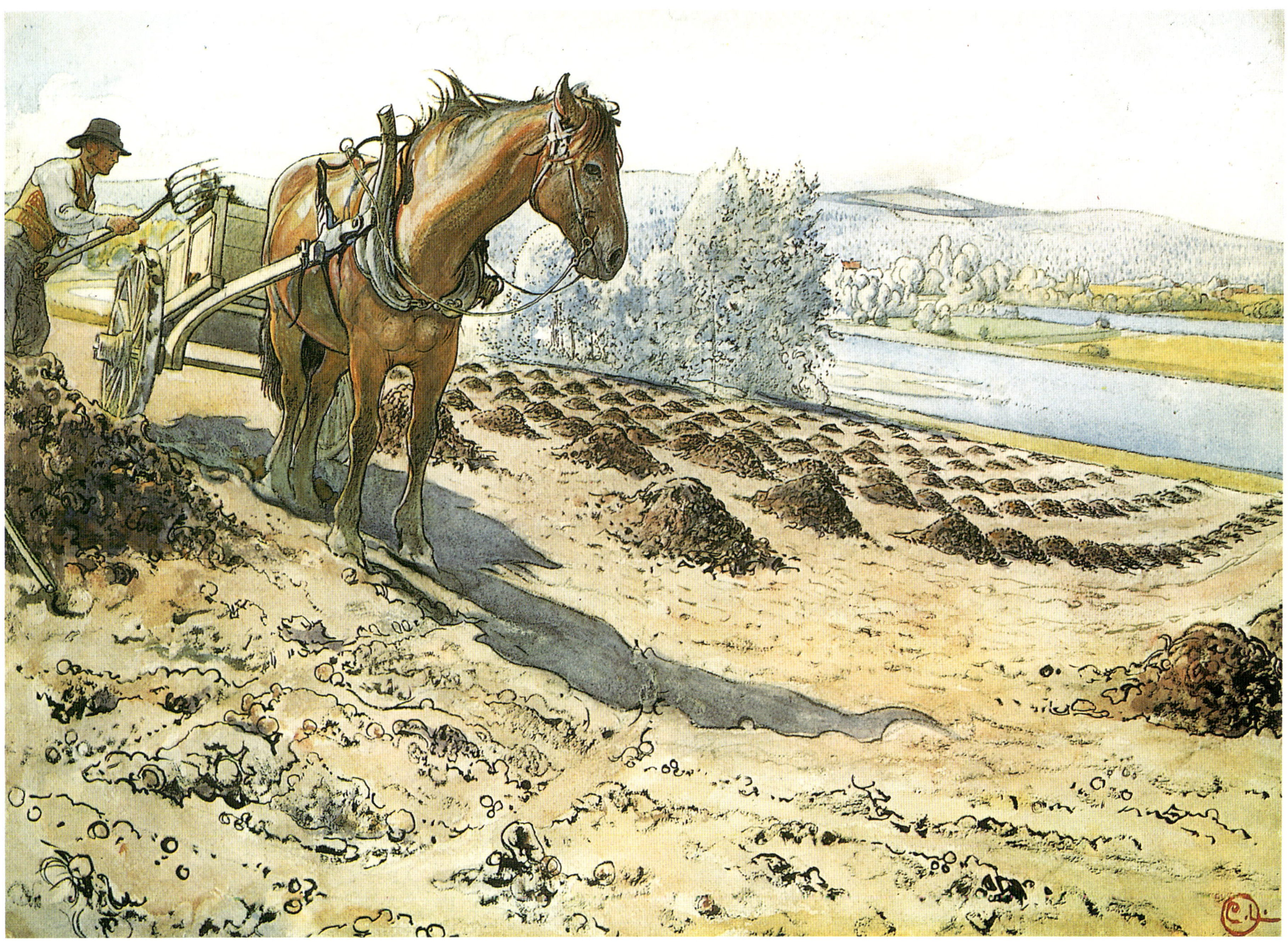

The arrival of September meant it was time for potato picking. Johan dug up a few potatoes first to see if they were ready for digging. He also kept a close eye on the weather: if the potato fields were wet and muddy, the work would take twice as long.

When a fine spell of weather came, the children got a last-minute holiday from school, because all hands were needed to pick the potatoes as quickly as possible. Johan hitched Brunte to the big farm wagon and loaded it up with a wooden plough and as many baskets and buckets as they could find. Then the women and children climbed in, and they all drove up to the potato hill. Brunte pulled the plough up one furrow and down the next, exposing the potatoes in the black soil. The children competed to see who could fill their bucket the quickest, and the women followed on behind, picking the potatoes the younger ones had missed, and using a hand hoe to uncover any still hidden in the ground.

In this painting, there are fourteen people working in the field. Everyone was paid according to what they had picked – including the children – and each one was given a sack of potatoes as well.

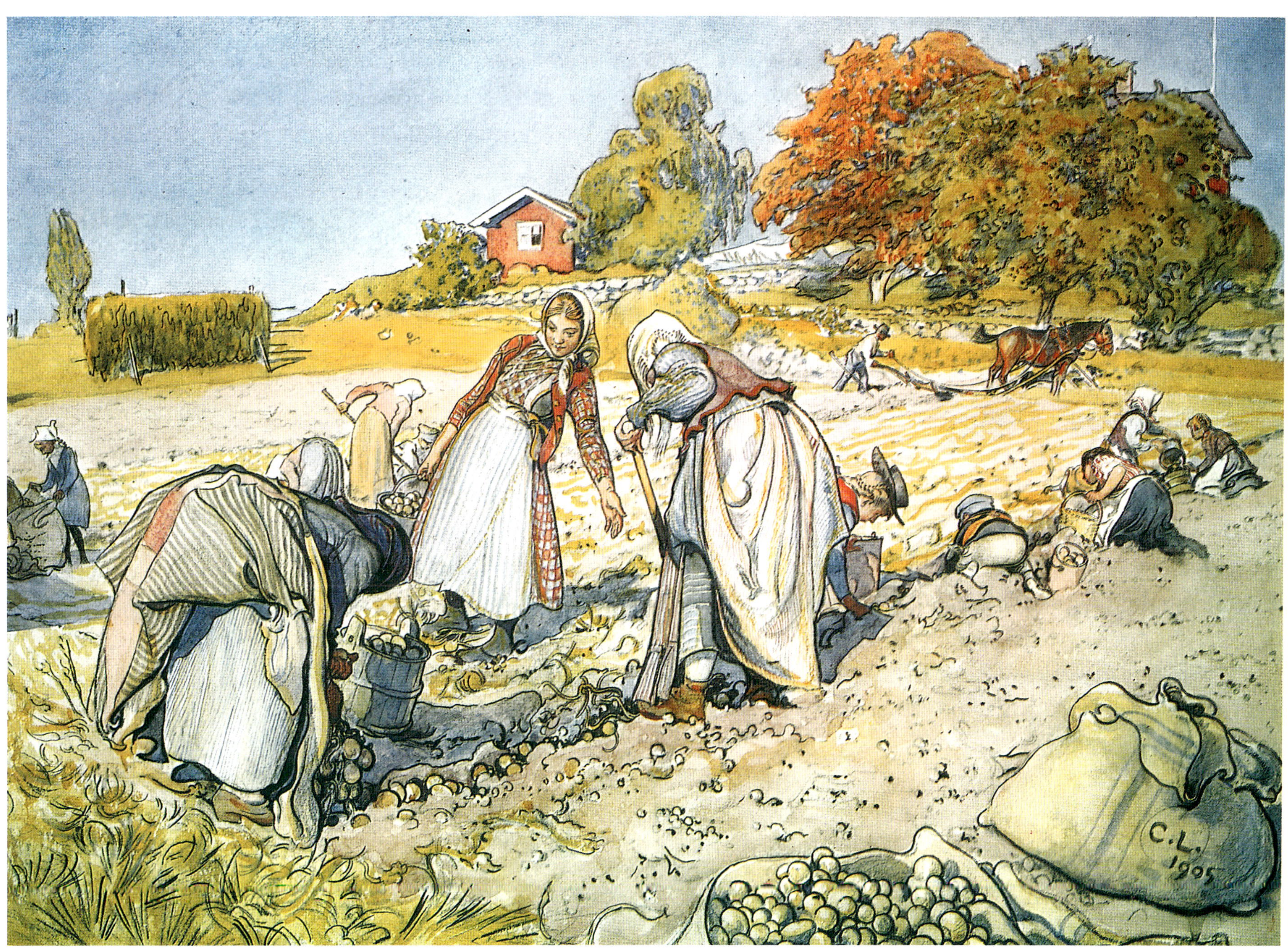
C.L.
1905

After the harvest was done, ploughing took up most of the time on the farm. In the first picture, Bäckström and Brunte are straining to plough furrows through the stubbly oat field. The second painting shows Johan and Bäckström digging ditches. As the autumn wore on, the weather worstened steadily and there was fog, and rain, and wind, and storms. The ditches were needed to stop the fields becoming waterlogged. It was back-breaking work. In later times, tile pipe would be laid under the soil for drainage so that the tractors and ploughs could go right across it.

There were lots of trees on the farm, and many were cut down to make charcoal to be sold for use in iron blast furnaces. In the third picture, Bäckström and Lisa have brought the farm's wood to Engström the charcoal-burner, who lived out in the woods. He lived on his own in his cabin, staying with the charcoal kiln because the fire could never be allowed to go out. For a few weeks each year, Bäckström lives with him, before returning to the farm covered in charcoal dust.

In the last painting it is December, and preparations have begun for Christmas celebrations. The butcher was brought to slaughter a pig, and they made ham and sausages, using all parts of the animal. Everyone set to work scouring and baking and decorating.

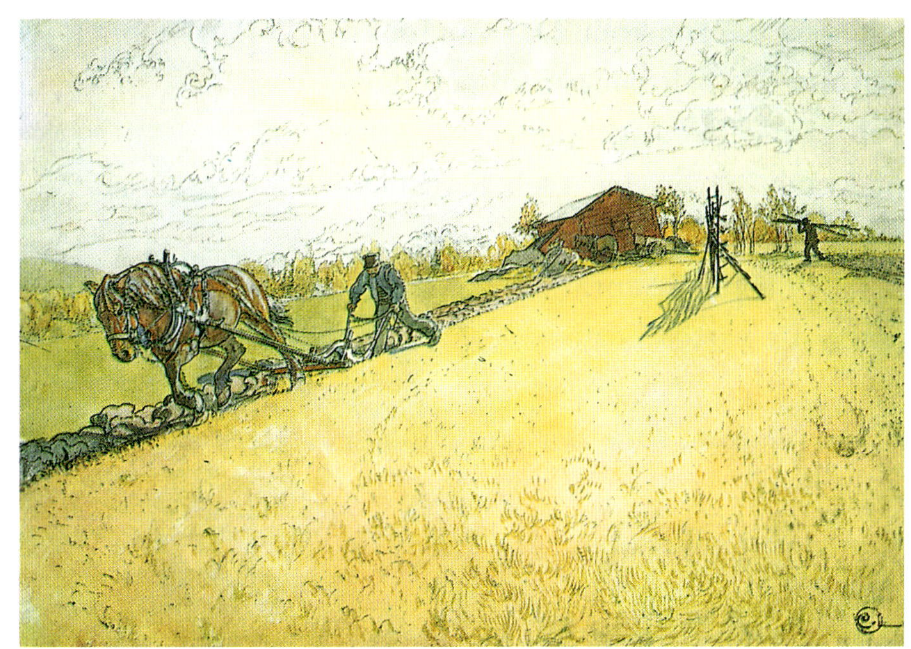
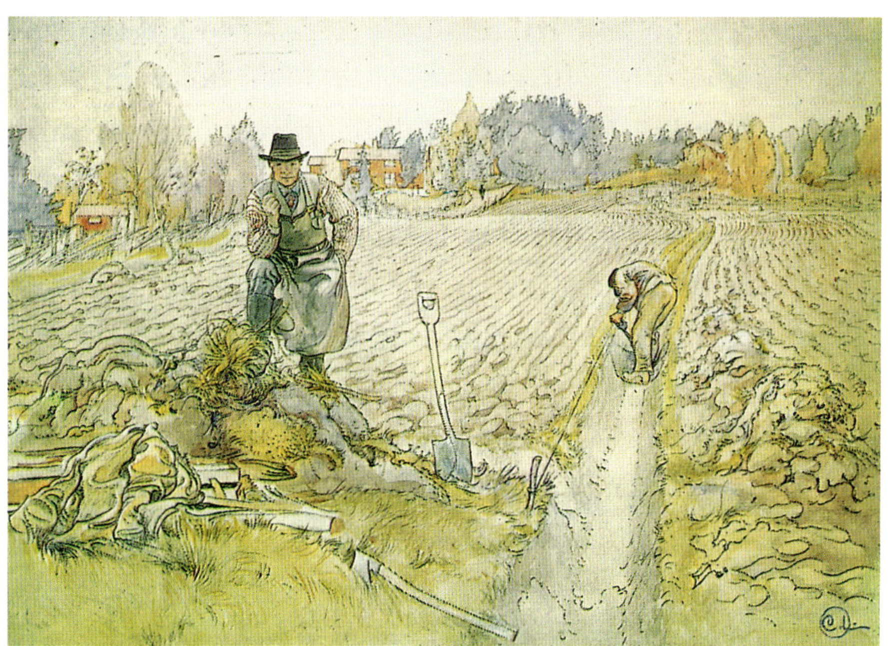
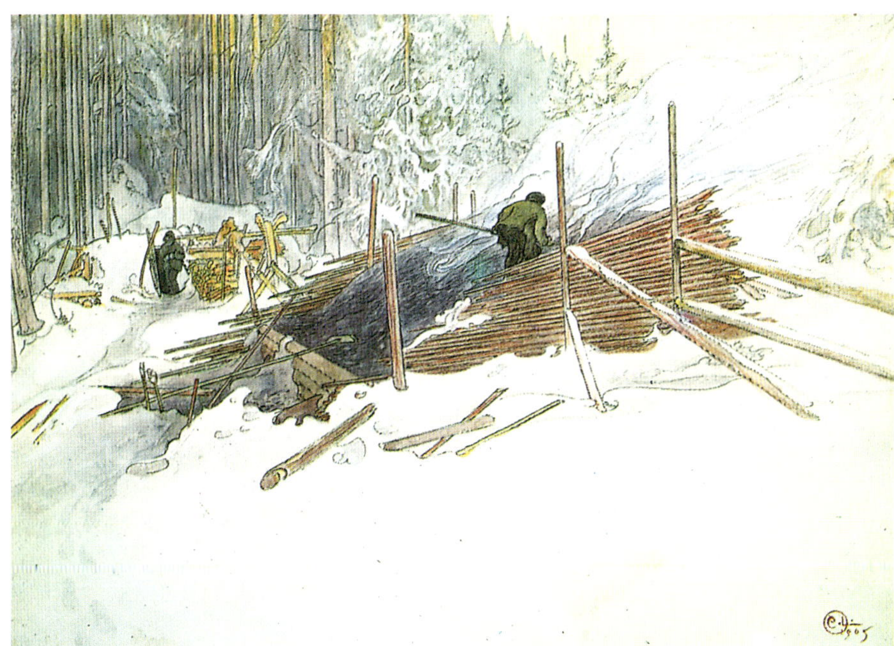
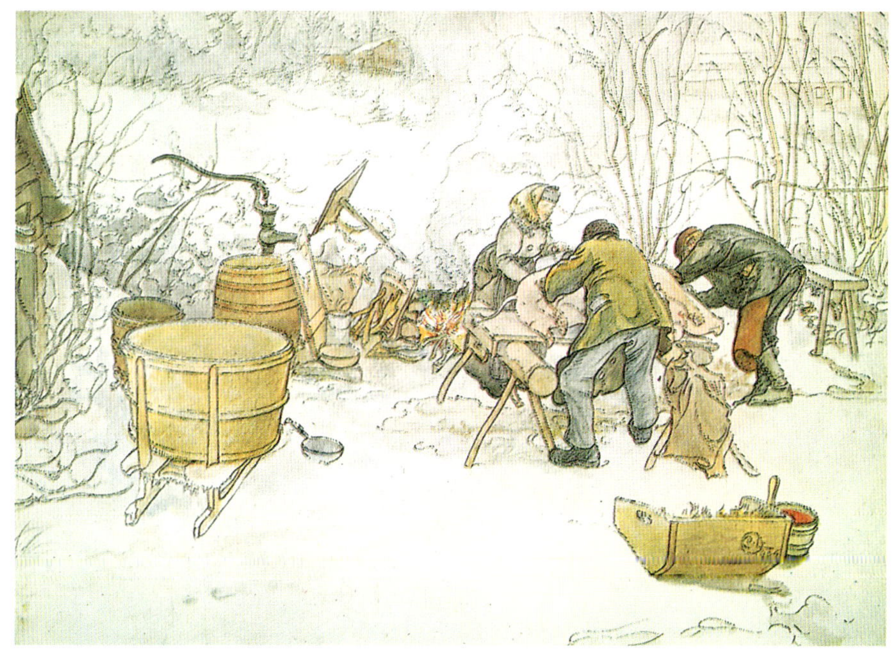

In this final painting, the results of a year's hard work on the farm are splendidly displayed. It is Christmas Eve, and all the guests have arrived at Lilla Hyttnäs: Johan and Johanna, Tekla, Bäckström and his wife, Elfström and Engström. Carl's father is seated in the large chair by the fire, carefully tended by Karin. Susanne and Lisbeth are giving out bread.

In the fire burns wood that Johan and Bäckström had cut the previous New Year. The tablecloth with the long fringed end was hand-made by Karin. All the food on the table came from Spadarvet, from the potatoes and the rye in the bread, to the butter, milk and cheese from the cows.

Carl Larsson himself was behind the easel, of course, sketching the scene as always. After they had eaten, Johan would play his violin, and they would dance all around the house before ending at the Christmas tree, and opening their presents.

In time, spring would come again and they would fish and sow and harrow. For today, they sat back and enjoyed the fruits of their labour.

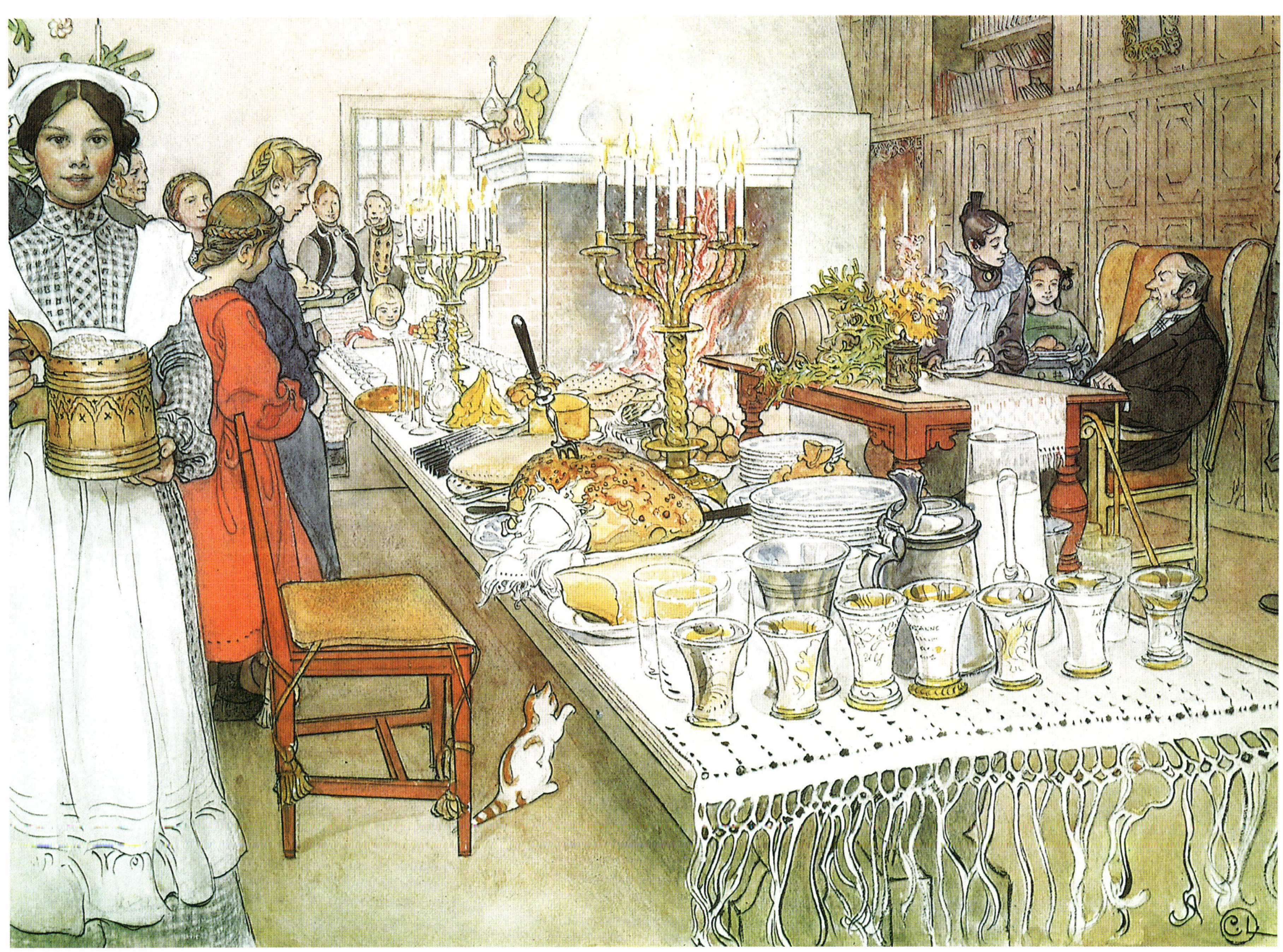

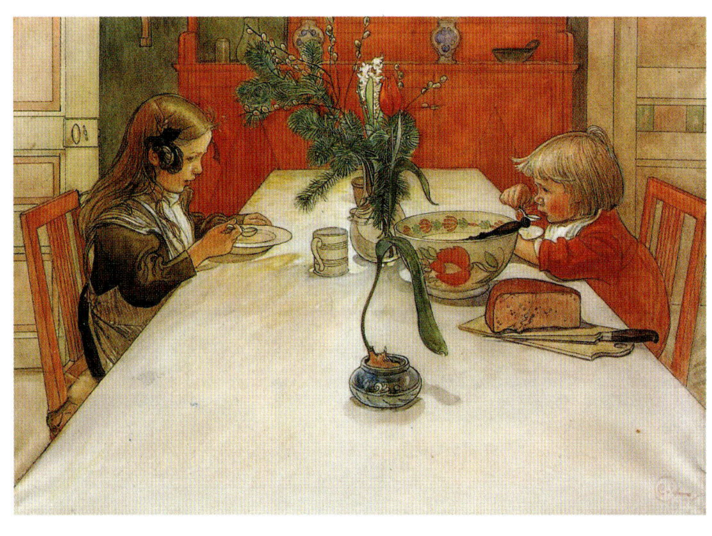

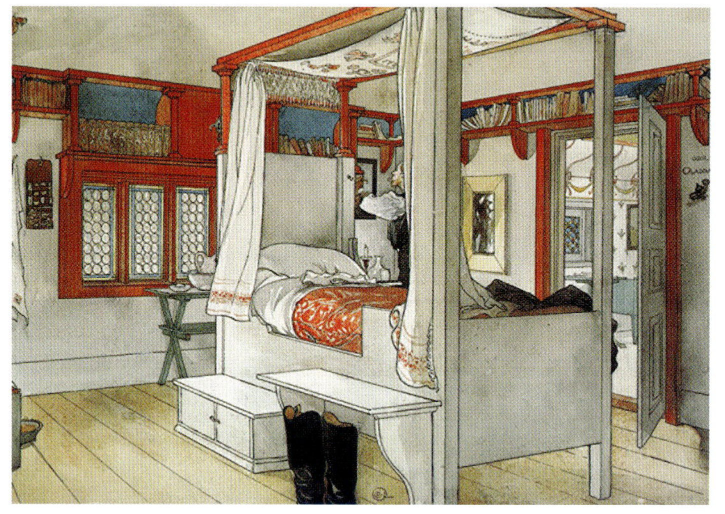

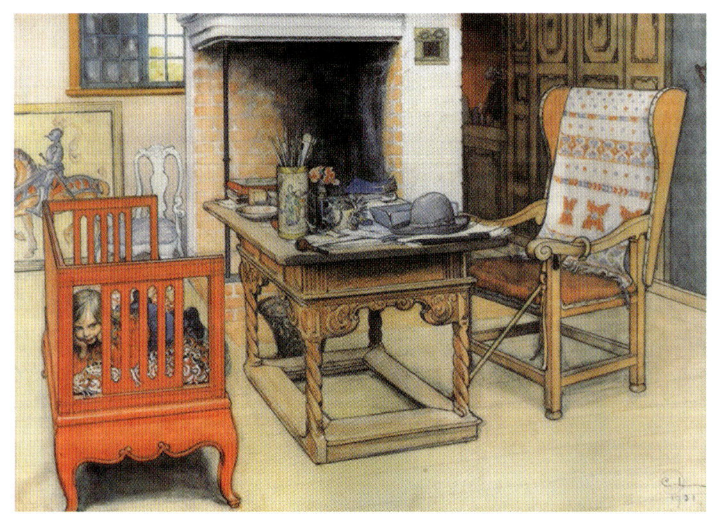

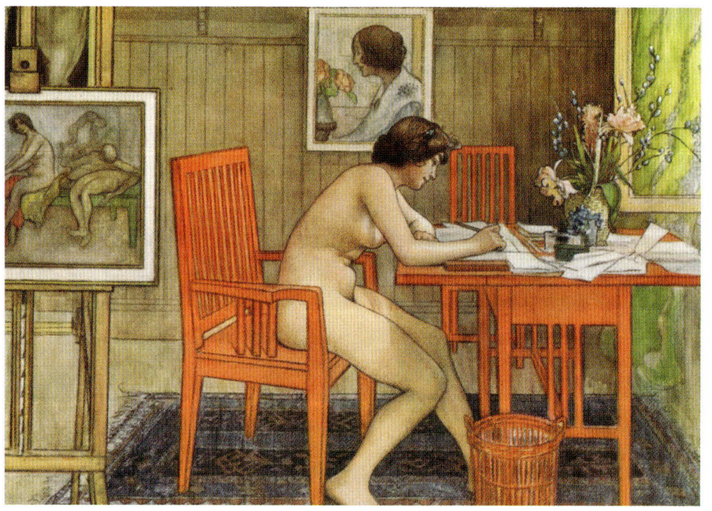

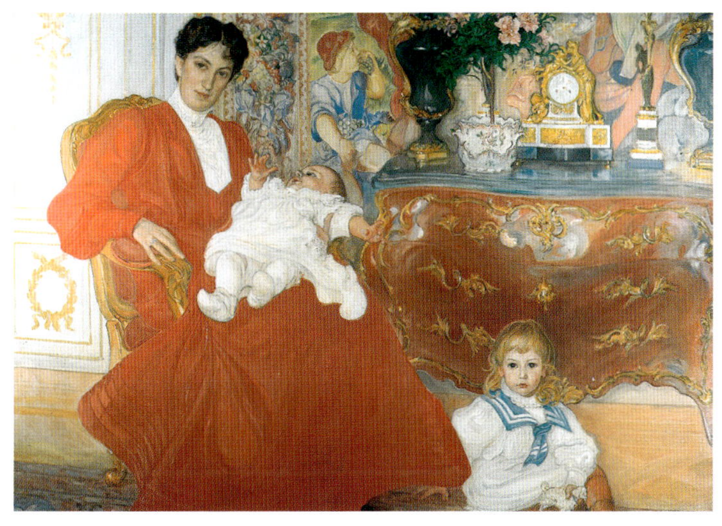

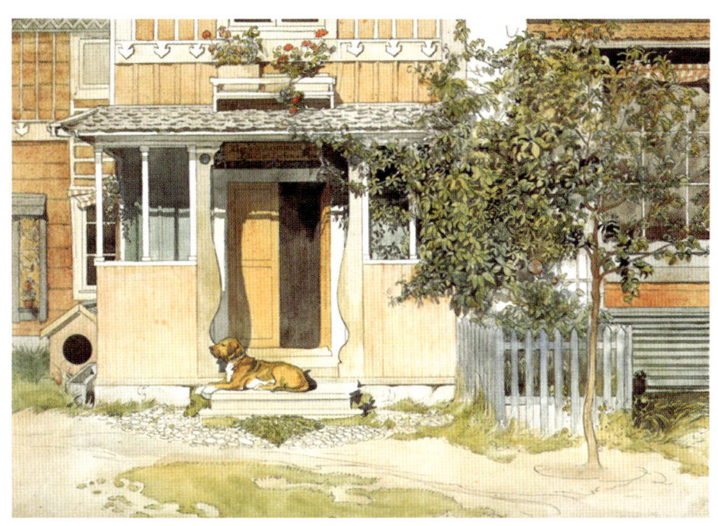

Selected additional work

Previous page

top left: *Evening Meal 1905*
top right: *Daddy's Room c.1895*
bottom left: *Peek-a-Boo 1901*
bottom right: *Model Writing Postcards 1906*

This page

top: *Mrs Dora Lammond and Her Two Eldest Sons 1903*
bottom: *The Verandah c.1895*

Trolls, Tomtes and Wicked Queens
A celebration of Swedish folklore by John Bauer

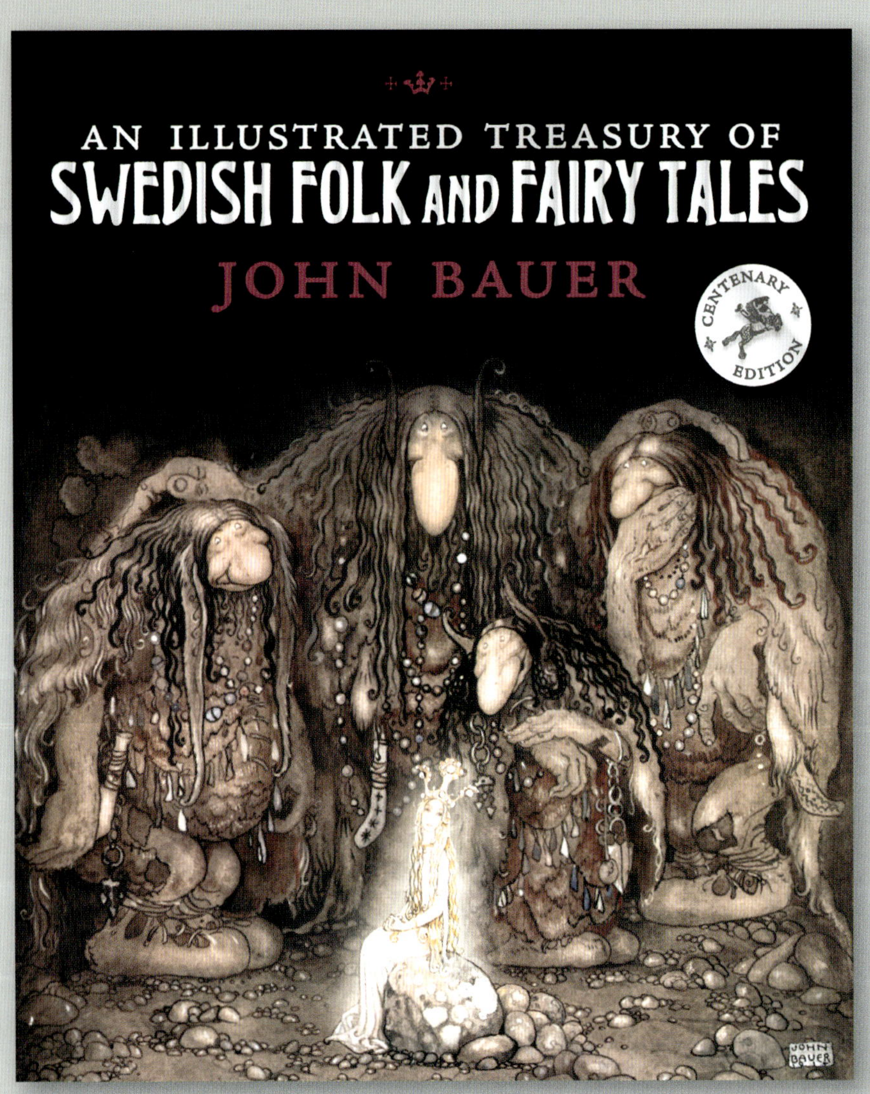

"A wonderful tribute to the visionary artist."
Youth Services Book Review

"A book to treasure."
Juno Magazine

Swedish artist John Bauer was one of the world's greatest illustrators of fairy tales. His art — renowned for its detail, character and subtle humour — has never looked more luminous and evocative than in this gorgeously produced edition which includes a wonderful illustrated biography of Bauer, celebrating his work and life one hundred years after his premature death.

With a foiled cover and ribbon marker, this treasury will be cherished for generations to come.

Cherished Children's Books from Sweden

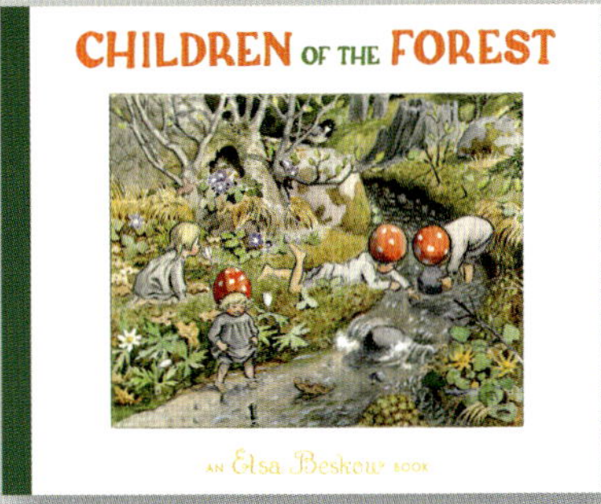

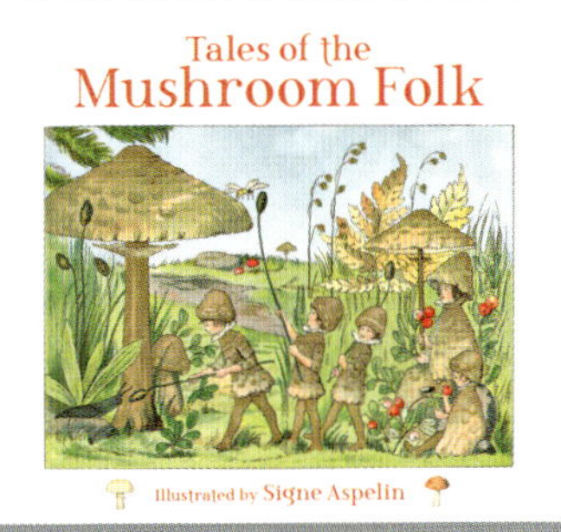

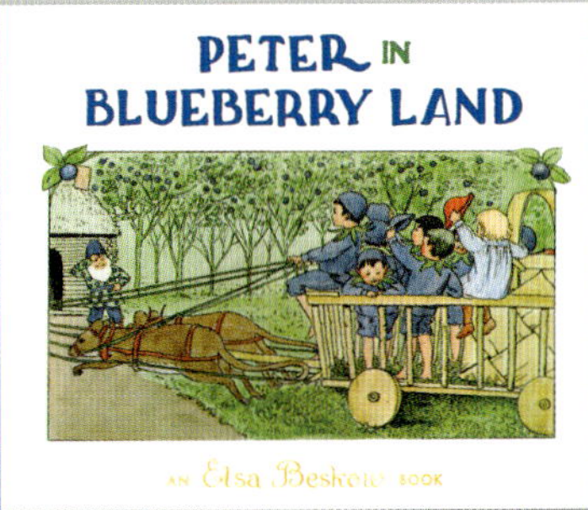

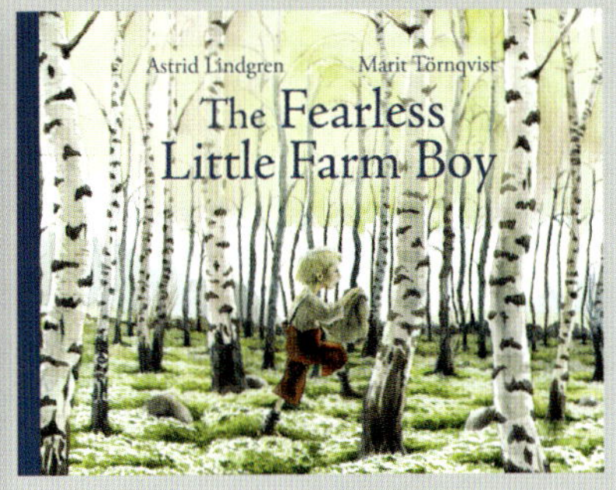

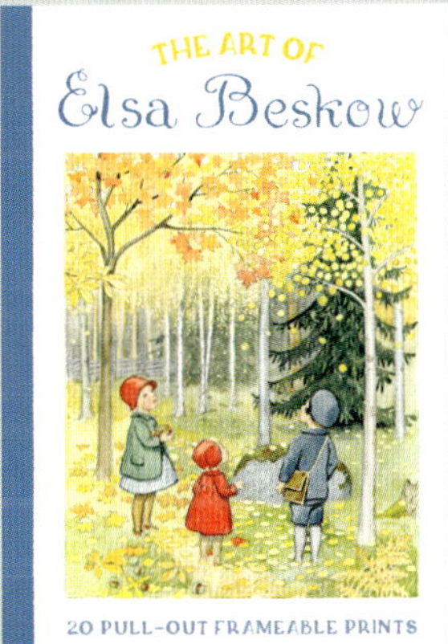

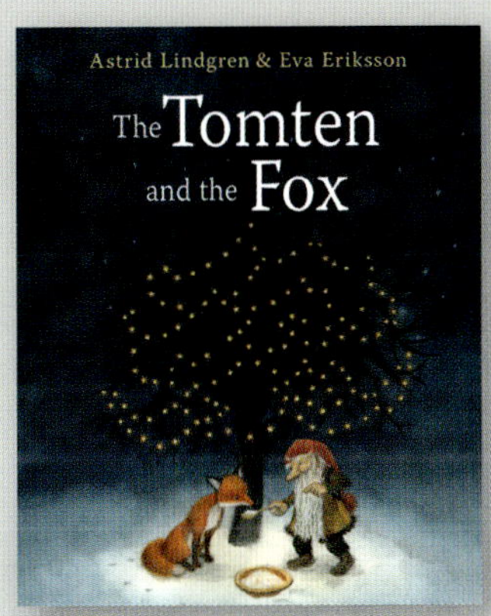

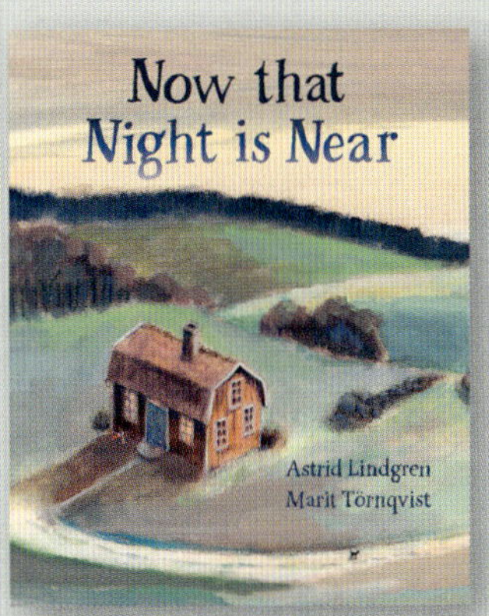

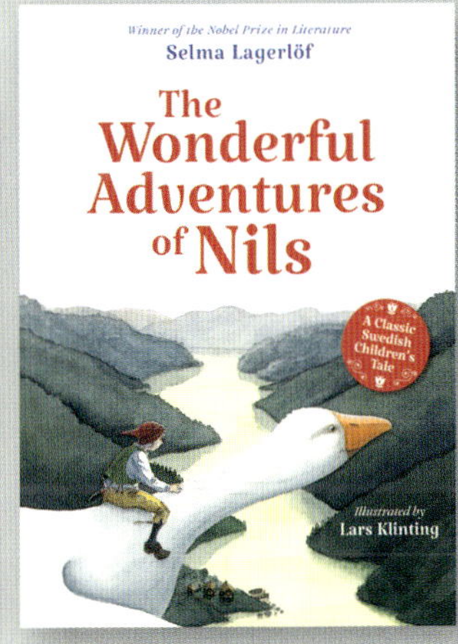

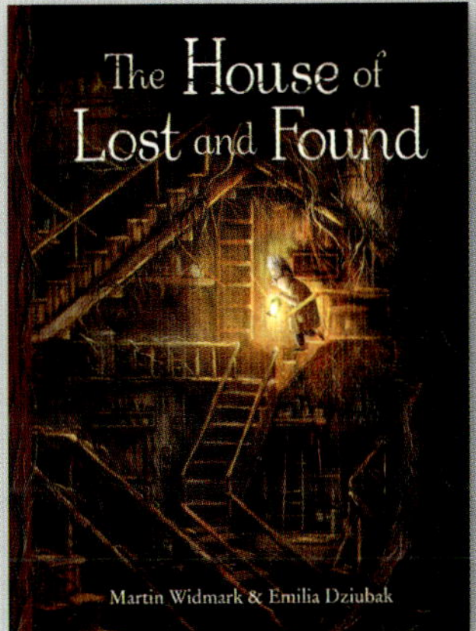

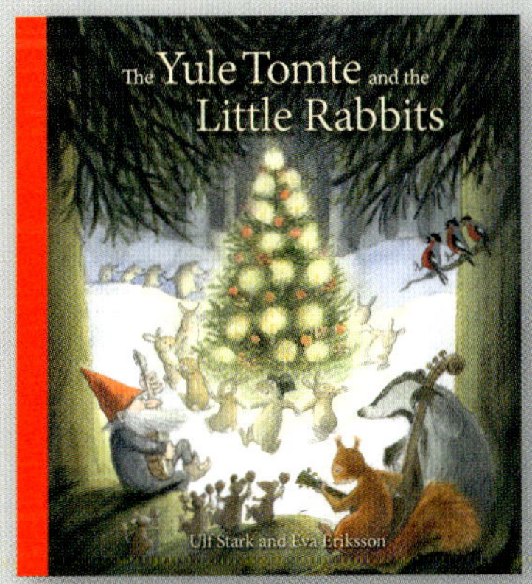

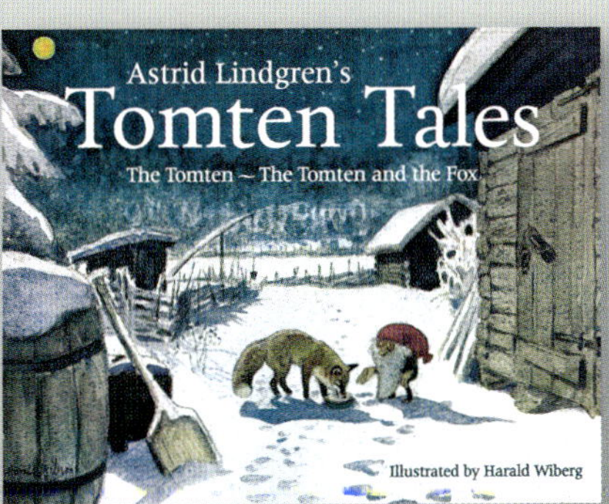

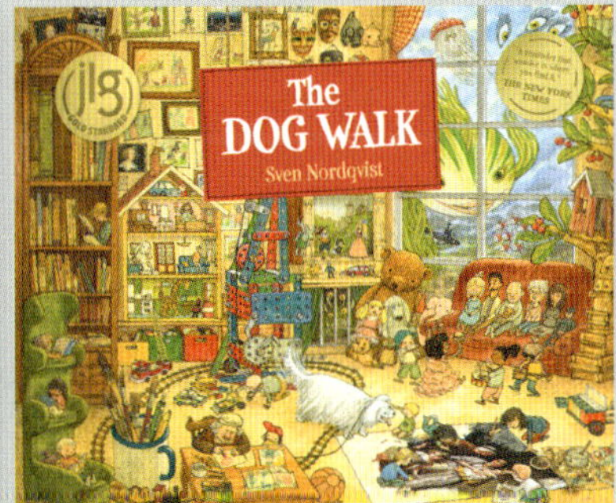

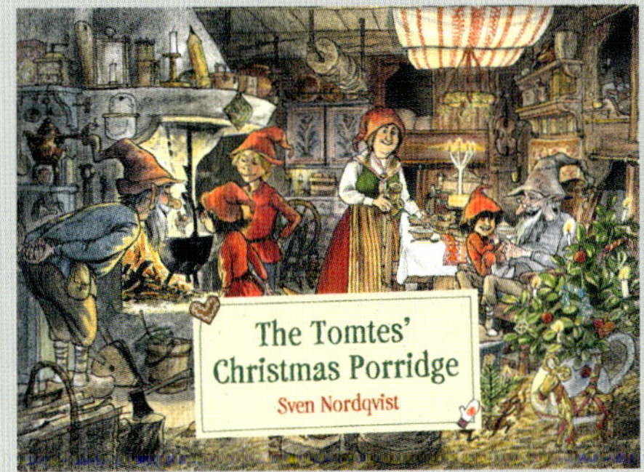

www.florisbooks.co.uk